Beyond Cheap Grace

A CALL TO RADICAL DISCIPLESHIP, INCARNATION, AND JUSTICE

Eldin Villafañe

William B. Eerdmans Publishing Company

Grand Rapids, Michigan / Cambridge, U.K.

Published 2006 by

Wm. B. Eerdmans Publishing Co.

255 Jefferson Ave. S.E., Grand Rapids, Michigan 49503 /

P.O. Box 163, Cambridge CB3 9PU U.K.

Printed in the United States of America

11 10 09 08 07 06   7 6 5 4 3 2 1

Library of Congress Cataloging-in-Publication Data

Villafañe, Eldin, 1940-

Beyond cheap grace: a call to radical discipleship, incarnation, and justice /
Eldin Willfañe.

p.   cm.

Includes bibliographical references.

ISBN-10: 0-8028-6323-X / ISBN-13: 978-0-8028-6323-2 (pbk.: alk. paper)

1. Grace (Theology) 2. Christian life. I. Title.

BT761.3.V55   2006

230′.994 — dc22

2006015451

www.eerdmans.com

BEYOND CHEAP GRACE

For

Sofía Pilar (b. 2003)

Bruce Jackson (1956-2002)

Edwin Villafañe (1938-2003)

Contents

CONTENTS

Foreword

As one of the nation's most influential Hispanic religious leaders, Dr. Eldin Villafañe is eminently qualified to address the subject of "radical discipleship, incarnation, and justice." Over the past three decades he has developed a distinguished national reputation through his work in the areas of urban ministry and theological education. His life's work and legacy represent a prophetic challenge and encouragement to all Christians to move "beyond cheap grace."

Under this familiar yet captivating rubric, Dr. Villafañe weaves together in these presentations the closely related theological themes of discipleship, incarnation, and justice. He does so in the form of three sermonic essays, using key biblical and historical reference points to challenge the church in America, theological education in the West, and Christian leadership in all cultures to be shaped by a theological mind-set that is deeply informed by the incarnation of Christ and clearly expressed in a cruciform life.

Dr. Villafañe brings to the work three presuppositions that inform his "call to radical discipleship, incarnation, and justice." They are drawn from the hymn of Christ in Philippians 2, the christological formulations of the early church, and the life of Amos in the Old Testament.

The first presupposition is that, according to Philippians 2, an extraordinary life is created by an extraordinary mind-set (the mind of Christ) that embraces "a practical moral reasoning willing to exercise a self-emptying." This is a christological-centered mind-set that molds human behavior into a life of costly discipleship, resulting in sacrifice and "parabolic actions."

The second presupposition is that the incarnation, as a frame of reference for theological reflection, has profound implications for the task of theological education. This incarnational perspective challenges the one-sided emphases (e.g., theory over practice) and entrenched dualisms (e.g., spiritual versus social) that are so deeply engrained in much of present-day theological education and leadership. Villafañe creatively develops an application of six christological perspectives from the early Christian period, showing how they both reveal the current imbalances in our theological curricula and inform the integrative mission of theological education globally and contextually. In doing so he seeks to display the full extent of the incarnational love of God.

The third presupposition is that a contextualized understanding and application of an incarnational theology calls for intrepid, courageous leaders who must have a depth of character formed by the essential qualities — a clear call from God, a sure word from God, and singular courage from God — to address the issues of social justice and spiritual transformation. The journey "beyond cheap grace" therefore involves bold leadership, rooted in the righteousness of God — called forth, informed, and inspired by God — to speak for and extend justice to all nations, and to purify the heart of God's people.

Dr. Villafañe's stimulating presentations, and the thoughtful responses that expand upon his themes, make this a very compelling and indeed indispensable volume for Christian leaders who care deeply about the theological mission of the church in our postmodern world. Its call to embrace justice and social concern as a constitutive part of a transformative gospel makes it an invaluable resource for all those whose vocation it is to advance the prophetic voice of theological education within our divided and violence-prone cultures, national and global. It will greatly benefit those Christian leaders and theological teachers who carry on their ministry at the intersection of the Christian church, the theological academy, and diverse cultural contexts; who desire to embrace unapologetically a robust, incarnational theology; and who act courageously to give expression to the cruciform life. To that end I highly commend this book.

HOWARD JOHN LOEWEN
Dean, School of Theology
Professor of Theology and Ethics
Fuller Theological Seminary

Preface

Self-denial in an affluent society is difficult. Some may even say it's "heretical" — not the posture of the King's Kids! We are constantly called by all kinds of media messages and images to a comfortable and self-satisfying life. This easy Christianity is even the melodious pitch of a "cross-less" church. Too often church programs and worship are geared to the entertainment and "event-full" gratification of its membership, while the preaching of the cross and the call to radical discipleship, incarnation, and justice are absent.

Yet, we cannot, we must not get away from the central figure of our faith: Jesus Christ. If we are his disciples, then his life and ministry must continue to inform our own. At the heart of Jesus' life and ministry stands the cross. The cross points both backward and forward. It points backward to Jesus' life of obedience, service, and sacrifice — a life identified with the poor and oppressed — in birth, teaching, ministry, and death. And it points forward to his church (his body) called to an equally cruciform life (Philippians 2). In the challenging words of Paul to the church at Philippi and to us: "For it has been granted to you on behalf of Christ not only to believe on him, but also to suffer for him" (Phil. 1:29, NIV). In the world we live in, the "obedience of faith" (Rom. 1:5; 16:26), which is another word for discipleship, is needed now more than ever. This "obedience of faith" is a costly discipleship that is informed by the cross and God's costly grace. This costly discipleship must characterize our Christian walk and ministry. Our churches and schools — all Christian institutions — must bear the marks of the incarnated and crucified God. Furthermore, this costly discipleship must manifest itself in an incarnational ministry of love and justice. Indeed, if Christians are to be faithful and to witness uncompromisingly to the reign of God over all creation, we must go "beyond cheap grace."

I want to thank Dean Howard J. Loewen of the School of Theology at Fuller Theological Seminary for the foreword to this book and the kind invitation to deliver the 2003-2004 Payton Lectures. This book represents the sermonic lectures I gave there in April 2004, which now I present as "sermonic essays" with very little revision of the text except for some added footnotes. I also wish to express my heartfelt thanks to the respondents to my lectures at Fuller and their contributions to the book: Richard Peace, a friend and former colleague at Gordon-Conwell Theological Seminary; Veli-Matti Kärkkäinen, a fellow Pentecostal scholar; and my colleague in the Latino struggle, Juan Francisco Martinez. "Muchas gracias mis amigos" for your participation in this project and your generous hospitality while at Fuller Theological Seminary.

I must note that the sermonic lectures/essays presented here were also speeches/sermons delivered at different venues in the past few years. They are also chapters found in my book in Spanish, *Fe, Espiritualidad y Justicia,* published by Palabra y más, San Juan, Puerto Rico. Of course, for the Payton Lectures and this book they represent an expanded and, I hope, improved thinking on the subject. It is my prayer that the Word of God may be heard through this humble effort at faithful witness and discipleship.

ELDIN VILLAFAÑE

The Christian Mind-set and Postmodernity: Lessons from Paul's Letter to the Philippians

Introduction

Being faithful to God's call to Christian discipleship is a costly business! The long list of Christian martyrs through church history gives ample testimony of the personal sacrifice of many. In that list one finds the young German theologian Dietrich Bonhoeffer. Among his works is the book, *The Cost of Discipleship*. In it Bonhoeffer has given us an expression or phrase that has grown in significance due, in no small part, to Bonhoeffer's own costly witness. I am referring to the phrase "cheap grace."

Listen to Bonhoeffer's words:

Cheap grace is the deadly enemy of our Church. We are fighting today for costly grace.

Cheap grace means grace sold on the market like cheapjack's wares. The sacraments, the forgiveness of sin, and the consolations of religion are thrown away at cut prices. . . .

Cheap grace is the preaching of forgiveness without requiring repentance, baptism without church discipline, communion without confession. . . . Cheap grace is grace without discipleship, grace without the cross, grace without Jesus Christ, living and incarnate. . . .

Costly grace is the gospel which must be sought again and again, the gift which must be asked for, the door at which a man must *knock*.

Such grace is *costly* because it calls us to follow, and it is *grace* because it calls us to follow *Jesus Christ*.[1]

"Cheap grace" is a phrase, and a concept, that has great theological meaning. In its practical sense, which I want to underline, it speaks to us of an "easy" Christianity. An easy Christianity is a Christianity that doesn't cost much, that pays no price. It thinks and says, in fact, "Please don't ask too much of me"; "Don't place any demands on me." "Cheap grace" portrays those persons who want to live in a secured comfort zone, those who think and say, "Do not disturb!" Ultimately, "cheap grace" characterizes that mode of thinking or mind-set that rejects obedience, commitment, discipleship, and the cross!

1. Dietrich Bonhoeffer, *The Cost of Discipleship* (New York: Touchstone, 1995), pp. 43-45.

- Such a Christianity cannot respond to the concerns and mind-set of our postmodern world.
- Such a Christianity has no attraction for a world in search of identity and meaning.
- Such a Christianity offers no hope to a hopeless world!
- Ultimately, such a Christianity is a scandal to the scandal of the cross!

Our contemporary society is experiencing, and lives in, the dismantling, the breakdown, of the promise of that seductive "siren" called *modernism*. In the succinct words of James F. Engel and William A. Dyrness, "The cry of Western civilization and the very essence of modernity became, 'There is no problem too big that it cannot be solved with human wisdom and technology.'"[2] The promises and power of modernism have been exposed for what they really are: an Enlightenment-era myth and utopian dream of a culture and civilization enamored with its intellectual and human constructs.

Dr. Samuel Pagán in a recent essay notes the following: "The modern project . . . with its absolute confidence in *science, liberty,* and *progress,* which was motivated by human autonomy under the dominion of reason, has been dismantling."[3]

---

2. James F. Engel and William A. Dyrness, *Changing the Mind of Missions: Where Have We Gone Wrong?* (Downers Grove, IL: InterVarsity Press, 2000), p. 59.

3. Samuel Pagán, "Entonces vi . . . una tierra nueva: De la modernidad a la postmodernidad en la iglesia hispana," *APUNTES* 20, no. 4 (2000): 137. See among the many works on postmodernity the fol-

More and more we are called to live in a culture and society characterized by that "slippery" term *postmodernity*. Postmodernity, with its radical skepticism about truth and knowledge and its radical suspicion of relationships of power, challenges the Christian and the church, more than ever, to *live* its faith. In view of this reality, the need of the hour is not for an easy Christianity, for cheap grace. The need of the hour is not for a soft, fragile, or fastidious Christianity, but for a rigorous, vigorous, concrete, and incarnated Christianity — a muscular Christianity, if you please — one that has the marks of the cross in its hands!

The challenge to the church in the twenty-first century is not just to speak the truth; the real challenge is to live the truth! As Christians we are called to incarnate the gospel, to live a life informed by the cross.

In a postmodern age, with its suspicion and skepticism, the words of St. Francis are very relevant: "Preach the gospel at all times; if necessary, use words."

lowing: Walter Anderson, *Reality Isn't What It Used to Be* (San Francisco: Harper and Row, 1990); Richard Bauckham, *Bible and Mission: Christian Witness in a Postmodern World* (Grand Rapids: Baker Academic, 2003); Zygmunt Bauman, *Life in Fragments: Essays in Postmodern Morality* (Oxford: Blackwell, 1995); Zygmunt Bauman, *Postmodern Ethics* (Oxford: Blackwell, 1993); Albert Borgmann, *Crossing the Postmodern Divide* (Chicago: University of Chicago Press, 1992); Justo L. González, "Metamodern Aliens in Postmodern Jerusalem," in *Hispanic/Latino Theology: Challenge and Promise,* ed. Ada María Isasi-Díaz and Fernando F. Segovia (Minneapolis: Fortress Press, 1996), pp. 340-50; Stanley J. Grenz, *A Primer on Postmodernism* (Grand Rapids: Eerdmans, 1996); Jean-François Lyotard, *The Postmodern Condition: A Report on Knowledge* (Minneapolis: University of Minnesota Press, 1984); and Harry Lee Poe, *Christian Witness in a Postmodern World* (Nashville: Abingdon Press, 2001).

In view of our postmodern reality, it is an imperative for the church and the seminary to teach and to live the implications of a theology of the incarnation and a theology of the cross. True Christian discipleship demands it. For at the heart of the gospel is the cross! The gospel is that meta-narrative, that grand story, of a crucified God. And as such, it responds to the critique of postmodernism that says that all meta-narratives oppress. Ours is the gospel of the apparent paradox — a crucified God who liberates!

My message can be summarized in the following two parts:

1. Postmodernity demands that Christians live a cruciform life in favor of the redemption of the world.
2. Stated pedantically, the shaping of a Christian *phronesis* (or thinking) is the *sine qua non* (or indispensable factor) for a *kenosis* (self-emptying) that results in a particular lifestyle, a cruciform and redemptive discipleship. Or, said in words from the Bronx (where I was raised), "You got to *think* differently to *act* differently, so as to make a *difference!*"

The Philippian Challenge

One of my favorite books of the Bible is Paul's epistle to the Philippians.[4] Its four chapters are very relevant for Chris-

4. Among many valuable works on Philippians, see the following:

5

tian discipleship. I believe that it has great lessons for us as we encounter a postmodern culture and society.

Paul, who founded the church in Philippi in his second missionary journey, around the years 49/50 of the Christian era, is a prisoner in Rome; the year is now around A.D. 61. While a prisoner, Paul receives from the church at Philippi an offering by way of Epaphroditus. Epaphroditus not only brings the offering but also brings news about the condition of Paul's beloved church in Philippi. The Philippians are suffering persecution in that city, which Luke reminds us was "a Roman colony and the leading city of that district of Macedonia" (Acts 16:12).[5] Philippi was a multicultural, complex, and quite sophisticated city — I dare say, not much different in its moral and spiritual needs and challenges than Boston, New York, Los Angeles, or even Pasadena!

In addition to the persecution from the outside, the church was experiencing disunity or discord within, among some distinguished members of the congregation. Given the circumstances, Paul decides to send words of consolation, encouragement, and exhortation. Paul writes the epis-

---

Efraín Agosto, "Paul vs. Empire: A Postcolonial and Latino Reading of Philippians," *PERSPECTIVAS* (Occasional Papers, Fall 2002), pp. 37-56; Gordon Fee, *Paul's Letter to the Philippians*, New International Commentary on the New Testament (Grand Rapids: Eerdmans, 1991); Karl Barth, *The Epistle to the Philippians* (Atlanta: John Knox Press, 1962); Moisés Silva, *Philippians*, Baker Exegetical Commentary on the New Testament (Grand Rapids: Baker Book House, 1992); and Peter O'Brien, *Commentary on Philippians*, New International Greek Testament Commentary (Grand Rapids: Eerdmans, 1991).

5. Here and throughout, biblical quotations are taken from the New International Version of the Bible, unless otherwise noted.

tle to the Philippians — a letter of friendship and a letter of moral exhortation.

In it Paul challenges the Philippians to "conduct yourselves in a manner worthy of the gospel of Christ" (Phil. 1:27) and of the "fellowship with the Spirit" (2:1) — vital words not only for the Philippians but also for us!

But above all Paul challenges them, and us, to a Christian mind-set — to the mind of Christ, a mind informed by the cross. This is a challenge that Paul underlines throughout the epistle and that he highlights in 2:5, when he exhorts them to "let this mind be in you, which was also in Christ Jesus" (KJV). The word "mind" is from the Greek *phroneo*, which means "think of," "be disposed," "attitude," or "mind-set." In Pauline strategy, and I may add divine strategy, this Greco-Roman city, like all our cities, needed a clear and concrete witness of the gospel of Jesus Christ — a witness that is the result or consequence of a Christian mind-set.

New Testament scholar Wayne Meeks, commenting on Philippians, reminds us that "This letter's most comprehensive purpose is the shaping of a Christian *phronesis*, a practical moral reasoning that is conformed to [Christ's] death in hope of his resurrection."[6] It is critical to understand that this *phronesis*, or Christian thinking, refers not only to one's thought process but also to the emotion and attitudes as well as to the ensuing lifestyle that proceeds from

6. Wayne A. Meeks, "The Man from Heaven in Paul's Letter to the Philippians," in *The Future of Early Christianity: Essays in Honor of Helmut Koester*, ed. Birger Pearson (Minneapolis: Fortress Press, 1991), p. 333.

them. *Phroneo* (thinking, attitude, or mind-set) is a distinctive Pauline term. Paul uses it ten times in this letter to the Philippians (Phil. 1:7; 2:2 [2 times]; 2:5; 3:15 [2 times]; 3:19; 4:2; and 4:10 [2 times]). It is important to remember here the words of Michael J. Gorman in his outstanding book *Cruciformity: Paul's Narrative Spirituality of the Cross:* "the purpose of Paul's letters generally, and the various kinds of narratives within them, is not to teach theology but to mold behavior, to affirm or — more often — to alter patterns of living, patterns of experience."[7]

In writing to his beloved church in Philippi, Paul knows that to overcome the discord inside the church and the persecution from the outside — and thus to be able to "conduct themselves worthy of the gospel of Christ" and express true discipleship — it was necessary for the Philippian Christians to have a renewed mind.

Several years ago, I had the honor of being the preacher at the celebration of the Centenary of the Union of the Presbyterian Church of New Zealand. One afternoon, while watching television, I noticed with interest the words of a "self-help guru" named Anthony Robbins. What called my attention was his expression, "What creates an extraordinary life is an extraordinary mind-set!" This is a great truth, but I prefer to paraphrase it to say, "What creates an extraordinary Christian life is an extraordinary mind-set — the mind of Christ!"

7. Michael J. Gorman, *Cruciformity: Paul's Narrative Spirituality of the Cross* (Grand Rapids: Eerdmans, 2001), p. 4.

From *Phronesis* to *Kenosis*

What is that *phronesis* or mind of Christ? How is this Christian mind-set expressed? These are pertinent questions!

> Your attitude [*phronesis*] should be the same as that
>   of Christ Jesus:
> Who, being in very nature God,
>   did not consider equality with God something
>   to be grasped,
> but made himself nothing,
>   taking the very nature of a servant,
>   being made in human likeness.
> And being found in appearance as a man,
>   he humbled himself
>   and became obedient to death — even death
>   on a cross!
>
> (Phil. 2:5-8)

In this passage, this hymn and declaration of faith of the primitive church,[8] the *phronesis* of Christ is manifested concretely and contextually — it incarnates itself. It expresses itself in a profound posture that in the Greek, in

---

8. See Gordon Fee, "Philippians 2:5-11: Hymn or Exalted Pauline Prose?" *Bulletin for Biblical Research* 2 (1992): 29-46; Jack T. Sanders, *The New Testament Christological Hymns* (Cambridge: Cambridge University Press, 1971); and Paul D. Feinberg, "The *Kenosis* and Christology: An Exegetical-Theological Analysis of Phil. 2:6-11," *Trinity Journal* 1 (1980): 21-46.

verse 7, is called *kenosis*. *Kenosis,* in this passage, is translated in various ways, for example, "made himself nothing," or "made himself of no reputation," or "emptied himself."

The meaning of *kenosis* or the "self-emptying" of Christ has been a debatable issue in Christology. Yet, most would agree that it involves at a minimum an emptying or giving up of certain prestige, prerogatives, and power by Christ. Christ takes the form of a man, becomes a servant, and humbles himself — he incarnates himself — thus identifying himself with us in bringing about our redemption through the cross.

The challenge to the church today — to Christian discipleship — is one that goes against the modern or postmodern mind-set: it is to have a Christian mind-set! It is to demonstrate a Christian *phronesis* by means of a *kenosis*. It is to make evident a Christian mind-set that is willing to exercise self-emptying — one that is willing to surrender its prestige, its prerogative, and, yes, its power in favor of redemptive and liberating purposes. The postmodern world is not looking for words — words can be cheap. The world is looking at you and me as Christians to show concrete acts of love and justice, to live a life that reflects the Master, the one who left his glory in heaven to identify with the poor, with the orphans and widows, with the sick and the brokenhearted, with the sinner — the one who climbed that cruel cross of Calvary for our salvation! The cry of the hour is for a Christianity that expresses the gospel of the reign of God in costly service, in sacrificial service — yes, in *costly discipleship!*

The Exemplary Paradigm

In Philippians 2, Paul not only challenges us to a Christian *phronesis* but also presents us with an exemplary paradigm. He gives us examples of Christian lives that show willingness to offer a costly service, a sacrificial ministry. Paul presents models of a cruciform life,[9] models of the mind of Christ — models of costly Christian discipleship.

Follow briefly with me this model or paradigm of Philippians 2. Note that there are four examples, four persons who demonstrate a costly service, a sacrificial ministry, a costly discipleship. This exemplary paradigm can be outlined in terms of four kinds of sacrificial service:

1. sacrifice of *soma* (or the body)
2. sacrifice of self-interest
3. sacrifice of self
4. supreme sacrifice

It is interesting to observe in these verses the way Paul uses, explicitly and implicitly, the words *sacrifice* and *service*. For after everything is said and done, in authentic Christian discipleship you can't have one without the other. Let's look at the passages in chapter 2 "backwards," that is, from the end of the chapter to the beginning.

The first person to consider is Epaphroditus (vv. 25-30). He represents the sacrifice of *soma* or the body.

---

9. On the cruciform life see the aforementioned work of Michael J. Gorman, *Cruciformity: Paul's Narrative Spirituality of the Cross.*

> But I think it is necessary to send back to you
> Epaphroditus, my brother, fellow worker and fellow
> soldier, who is also your messenger, whom you sent
> to take care of my needs. For he longs for all of you
> and is distressed because you heard he was ill. In-
> deed he was ill, and almost died. But God had mercy
> on him, and not on him only but also on me, to spare
> me sorrow upon sorrow. Therefore I am all the more
> eager to send him, so that when you see him again
> you may be glad and I may have less anxiety. Wel-
> come him in the Lord with great joy, and honor men
> like him, because he almost died for the work of
> Christ, risking his life to make up for the help you
> could not give me.

Epaphroditus represents costly discipleship by being willing to risk his health, his body, for the gospel.

The second person to consider is Timothy (vv. 19-22).
He represents the sacrifice of self-interest. Listen to Paul's
words:

> I hope in the Lord Jesus to send Timothy to you
> soon, that I also may be cheered when I receive news
> about you. I have no one else like him, who takes a
> genuine interest in your welfare. For everyone looks
> out for his own interests, not those of Jesus Christ.

Timothy represents costly discipleship by being willing to
risk his self-interest for the gospel.

The third person is Paul (vv. 17-18). He represents the sacrifice of self.

> But even if I am being poured out like a drink offering on the sacrifice and service coming from your faith, I am glad and rejoice with all of you. So you too should be glad and rejoice with me.

Paul represents costly discipleship by being willing to risk himself — his total life — for the gospel.

And the fourth person is Jesus (vv. 5-11). He represents the supreme sacrifice.

> Your attitude [*phronesis*] should be the same as that
>   of Christ Jesus:
> Who, being in very nature God,
>   did not consider equality with God something
>   to be grasped,
> but made himself nothing,
>   taking the very nature of a servant,
>   being made in human likeness.
> And being found in appearance as a man,
>   he humbled himself
>   and became obedient to death — even death
>   on a cross!
> Therefore God exalted him to the highest place
>   and gave him the name that is above every name,
> that at the name of Jesus every knee should bow,
>   in heaven and on earth and under the earth,

and every tongue confess that Jesus Christ is Lord,
    to the glory of God the Father.

Jesus represents the supreme sacrifice — the ultimate cost of discipleship!

An important point to note here is that this sacrificial or costly discipleship is not given in a masochistic or oppressive spirit. On the contrary, it is rendered in a spirit saturated by joy! In this letter of only four chapters, the word *joy* is found about sixteen times. Paul wants to remind the Philippians, and he also wants to remind us, that through the power of the Holy Spirit our costly discipleship in Christ is imbued with, penetrated by, and saturated with joy. Or it should be! This exemplary paradigm must inform our discipleship. Paul knows full well that our obedience to "do everything . . . in a crooked and depraved generation [will result in our shining] like stars in the universe" (Phil. 2:14-15).

This exemplary paradigm underlines the truth that service to the Lord involves sacrifice. Nevertheless, our sacrificial service, our costly discipleship, when done in the Spirit, is "a fragrant offering, an acceptable sacrifice, pleasing to God" (Phil. 4:18).

As we are reminded by Karl Barth, "In many of the New Testament records the call to discipleship closes with the demand that the disciple should take up his cross. This final order crowns, as it were, the whole call, just as the cross of Jesus crowns the life of the Son of Man."[10] Or, as it is expressed by

10. Karl Barth, *The Call to Discipleship* (Minneapolis: Fortress Press, 2003), p. 67; this volume is based on Karl Barth's *Church Dogmatics* IV/2.

Richard Peace, commenting on discipleship in Mark's Gospel in his superb study *Conversion in the New Testament*, "As the Master, so the disciple. *The pattern which the Son of Man will live out is the pattern that his disciples must follow.*"[11]

In the postmodern epoch that we must live in, the gospel needs to be incarnated in costly discipleship. The world looks at the church and wants to see in our lives the marks of the cross — not the search for comfort, prestige, power, or fame. Christian discipleship is costly! I do not know what is or will be the cost or sacrifice that you will pay. But let me assure you that success, faithfulness to your call, will demand sacrifice.

The great theological ethicist Paul Lehmann, following Karl Barth, speaks of the challenges to individual Christians and to the church to take "parabolic action" in the world.[12] You see, our acts of costly service in the world are "parabolic actions." Like the parables of the New Testament, such actions express the "mind of Christ" and the secret or mystery of the kingdom of God. Our "parabolic actions" are witnesses to the truth before a world that would read our costly service, our costly discipleship, and, with the help of God, understand "that [we] are a letter of Christ . . . written not with ink but with the Spirit of the living God" (2 Cor. 3:3).

In a chapter entitled "Witness to the Truth in a Postmodern and Globalized World," in his small but powerful

---

11. Richard V. Peace, *Conversion in the New Testament: Paul and the Twelve* (Grand Rapids: Eerdmans, 1999), p. 254 (his emphasis).

12. Paul Lehmann, *Ethics in a Christian Context* (New York: Harper & Row, 1963), p. 122; see also pp. 74-101.

little book *Bible and Mission: Christian Witness in a Postmodern World*, Richard Bauckham states:

> The image the Bible itself often suggests for the way its truth is to be claimed is that of witness. This is an extremely valuable image with which to meet the postmodern suspicion of all metanarratives as oppressive. Witness is non-coercive. It has no power but the convincingness of the truth to which it witnesses. Witnesses are not expected, like lawyers, to persuade by the rhetorical power of their speeches, but simply to testify to the truth for which they are qualified to give evidence. But to be adequate witness to the truth of God and the world, witness must be a *lived witness involving the whole of life and even death*. And as such it can show itself to be not self-serving.[13]

Conclusion

Let me underscore, in summary, certain salient points of my message about how we Christians must live in a postmodern world.

- We have to overcome "cheap grace," which is a scandal to the "scandal of the cross."

13. Richard Bauckham, *Bible and Mission: Christian Witness in a Postmodern World* (Grand Rapids: Baker Academic, 2003), p. 99 (my emphasis).

- The truth of the gospel must be lived; it must incarnate itself in concrete acts of love and justice.
- We are called to a Christian *phronesis* — to the mind of Christ.
- This Christian *phronesis* is expressed in *kenosis,* in self-emptying of prestige, prerogatives, and power.
- We are called to render a costly discipleship, to live a cruciform life.
- Costly discipleship is evidence of and motivation for a Christian *phronesis.*
- Our sacrificial service, our costly discipleship in society, is made up of "parabolic actions," concrete witnesses to the truth of divine love and grace.

I conclude with words of exhortation and of prayer; they are words of Paul to the Romans, but also to you and me:

Therefore, I urge you, brothers [and sisters], in view of God's mercy, to offer your bodies as living sacrifices, holy and pleasing to God — which is your spiritual [or reasonable] worship. Do not conform any longer to the pattern of this world, but be transformed by the renewing of your mind. Then you will be able to test and approve what God's will is — his good, pleasing and perfect will. (Rom. 12:1-2)

"The Christian Mind-set and Postmodernity"

Richard Peace

It is an honor to be able to respond to this fine sermonic essay by my friend Dr. Eldin Villafañe. Dr. Villafañe and I taught together for many years at Gordon-Conwell Theological Seminary. I watched as he developed the groundbreaking Center for Urban Ministerial Education (CUME) in Boston, and I had the privilege of teaching a number of classes there. On one occasion we traveled together for three weeks in Brazil as part of an Association of Theological Schools (ATS) study tour.

In his first essay he has brought to our attention key themes that are at the heart of our concerns: the contemporary church, postmodernity, discipleship, and the epistle to the Philippians. As he addressed these themes, I found myself saying yes to his perceptive call, to what he calls a cross-oriented lifestyle guided by the mind of Christ. So what I will seek to do in this response, rather than argue with Dr. Villafañe, as is sometimes the role of a respondent, is to amplify what he has said and add a few of my own observations to some of his key points.

The Problem in the Church

First, I want to interact with the problem that Dr. Villafañe identifies in the contemporary church. Diagnosis is crucial, as William Abraham points out in his book *The Logic of Renewal:*

> Proposals about renewal invariably follow a simple pattern. They propose a *description* of the life of the church that depicts what is flawed in one way or another — we are told that the church is diseased or sick in some crucial respect. This leads to a *diagnosis* as to why the flaw or set of flaws has developed — we are given an account of the etiology of the sickness of the church. Finally, there is a *prescription* as to how to put things right — we are offered an account of the medicine that we need to take if the church is to be cured. . . . [But] renewal can go wrong in all sorts of ways. It can go wrong because of the original mis-description, because of misdiagnosis, or because the doctor has prescribed the wrong medicine. . . . It can all too easily lead to the killing of the patient.[1]

1. William J. Abraham, *The Logic of Renewal* (Grand Rapids: Eerdmans, 2003), pp. 3-4.

Abraham identifies a variety of proposals that have been offered in recent years for renewal in the church, ranging from fundamentalists, like James Draper, who want to get us back to a proper view of the Bible; to charismatics, such as Dennis Bennett, who want us to have a fresh encounter with the Holy Spirit; to Bishop Spong, who thinks the fundamental problem of the church is intellectual, that we are wedded to a set of intellectual commitments that he feels are no longer viable; to Cardinal Ratzinger (now Pope Benedict XVI), who thinks the church will be renewed if we accept the primacy of Peter and hence papal authority. In fact, Abraham identifies some fourteen options for renewal, including one by former Fuller faculty member Peter Wagner, who argues that renewal of the church as it exists is not possible, that we need to begin a whole new church, an apostolic church, headed by apostles. Peter Wagner identifies himself as "the presiding apostle of the International Coalition of apostles." So accurate description and correct diagnosis are crucial.

Dr. Villafañe asserts that *cheap grace* is the problem, borrowing from the thinking of Dietrich Bonhoeffer. And indeed, contemporary Christianity has become a low-demand kind of enterprise:

"Come to church," we say, "we will entertain you."
"We will give you good worship," by which we mean
music you like so that you can feel close to God.
"We will help you with your relationships."
"All you have to do is come."
"We won't demand anything much from you."

A Response to "The Christian Mind-set and Postmodernity"

George Gallup Jr. would agree with this diagnosis:

> Who cannot point to gaps in what Americans believe
> and how they behave? . . . In polls on biblical literacy,
> half of those describing themselves as Christians are
> unable to name who delivered the Sermon on the
> Mount. Many Americans cannot name the reason
> for celebrating Easter or what the Ten Command-
> ments are. People think the name of Noah's wife was
> Joan, as in *Joan of Ark.* . . .
>
> And should not a nation begun in the spirit of
> One who called people to love God and love neighbor
> show more humane progress? Our economic stan-
> dard of living continues to rise, but few would argue
> that our compassion index has soared. The gap be-
> tween the comfortably wealthy and the needy poor
> widens. . . .
>
> Between what Americans profess and manifest
> lie gaps of knowledge, behavior and ethics. When
> our nation's four to five hundred thousand clergy ad-
> dress their congregations each week, they face peo-
> ple whose choices contradict their values. . . . Clergy
> preach to boomers who believe in angels but cheat
> on taxes, college students who pray but regularly get
> drunk.[2]

2. George Gallup Jr. and Timothy Jones, *The Next American Spiritual-ity: Finding God in the Twenty-First Century* (Colorado Springs, CO: Char-iot Victor Publishing, 2000), pp. 30-33.

It does not take a Gallup to notice this disconnect between belief and lifestyle. As Dr. Villafañe points out, the postmodern world is not impressed by such a disconnect.

The Emerging Church

Let us think about the contemporary church and some of the new models for church that are emerging in response to the very problem named by Dr. Villafañe. During the decade of the 1990s, the paradigm for the church, which garnered a lot of attention, was that of the so-called seeker-sensitive church. The idea is to build a church around the issues, tastes, and needs of non-members and then draw them to church so we can teach them about Jesus. This is a strategy that worked. We grew large seeker-sensitive churches, a number of which are here in southern California.

Without impugning the motives or even challenging the assumptions of the seeker churches, suffice it to say that Generation X is having none of this. Gen X never much liked the boomer enterprise, so they fled quietly from boomer churches. Now they have come of age as a generation. Gen X is, roughly speaking, the twenty- and thirty-somethings. They are putting together their own communities of faith, and these look quite different from seeker churches. They are more transformational churches than informational churches, more missional churches than attractional churches (to use phrases I first heard from Dr. Ryan Bolger here at Fuller).

For want of a better title, this movement is being called the "emerging church." Such churches are, for the most part, smaller than seeker churches; they feature intense community and are actively involved in the arts and in ministries of compassion. They are concerned for worship innovation and liturgy and are more apt to be informed by missional church thinking than by purpose-driven thinking.

I have just been reading a book by Doug Pagitt entitled *Reimagining Spiritual Formation,* in which he talks about Solomon's Porch Community and what he describes as "an experimental church" in Minneapolis. Solomon's Porch is an Evangelical Covenant Church plant. The Evangelical Covenant, of all denominations, is trying to stay open to the postmodern generation. Who would have thought that free-church Scandinavians would encourage new church plants that are both experimental and multiethnic?

In any case, Solomon's Porch is an attempt to put together a church focused on communal spirituality. In their own words, they are concerned about Christian formation that goes beyond the educational model of Christian discipleship, one that seeks to bring the whole of life into the orb of Christ.

Here is how Doug Pagitt describes the various spiritualities that make up Solomon's Porch:

At Solomon's Porch we are seeking a spiritual formation that, in its essence, is not about individual effort but communal action involving a *spirituality of physi-*

cality, centered on the way we lead our lives, allowing us to be Christian in and with our bodies and not in our minds and hearts only; a *spirituality of dialogue* within communities where the goal is not acquiring knowledge, but spurring one another on to new ways of imagining and learning; a *spirituality of hospitality* that is not limited to food before or after meetings but is intended to create an environment of love and connectedness where people are formed and shaped as they serve and are served by one another; a *spirituality of the knowledge of God* where the Bible is not reduced to a book from which we extract truth, but the Bible is a full, living, and active member of our community that is listened to on all topics of which it speaks; a *spirituality of creativity* where creative gifts are not used as content support but rather as an invitation for those so inclined to participate in the generative processes of God; a *spirituality of service,* which is the natural response of all seeking to live in the way of Jesus and is not reserved for the elite of the faith.[3]

Is this movement perhaps, at least in part, an attempt to embody *phronesis* and *kenosis,* a self-emptying lifestyle of giving based on the mind of Christ, as Dr. Villafañe has urged? Solomon's Porch would probably agree that they are

3. Doug Pagitt, *Reimagining Spiritual Formation: A Week in the Life of an Experimental Church* (Grand Rapids: Zondervan, 2004), p. 32.

attempting to do something like this, though they would use different language. They certainly work on the whole issue of developing the mind of Christ. As they do this, they would assert that correct thinking goes beyond mere information. "Information alone rarely suffices to create belief," as Pagitt puts it.[4] Like everything else in Solomon's Porch, belief emerges out of community as together they engage in a deep reading of Scripture, which is then tried on and tried out, and thus gives life to the community. Belief is lived belief, just what Dr. Villafañe calls for.

Suffering Is at the Heart of Spirituality

At the heart of such lived belief is suffering. Suffering is a key facet of Gen X spirituality. In fact, according to Tom Beaudoin in his book *Virtual Faith*, suffering is one of the four defining marks of Gen X spirituality:

"Institutions Are Suspect"
"Experience Is Key"
"Suffering Has a Religious Dimension"
"Ambiguity Is Central to Faith."[5]

This makes sense, given that there is much suffering in Generation X. Remember who these folks are: the forgotten

4. Pagitt, *Reimagining Spiritual Formation*, p. 115.
5. Tom Beaudoin, *Virtual Faith: The Irreverent Spiritual Quest of Generation X* (San Francisco: Jossey-Bass, 1998), the titles of chapters 4-7.

generation, overshadowed, outnumbered, and underappreciated by their boomer parents, who called them whiners and slackers. They were the original latch-key kids, who raised themselves with the help of television, the electronic baby sitter, because both Mom and Dad had to work. They are the most aborted generation in history. They are children of divorce; the divorce rate shot up to 50 percent in their parents' generation. Yes, Gen X knows about suffering. So in many ways the letter to the Philippians is their letter — joy in the midst of suffering, as Dr. Villafañe has pointed out.

I am always struck by the fact that this letter in which joy is so central was written while Paul was incarcerated, possibly under house arrest and chained day and night to an ever-changing coterie of palace guards. Paul does suffer: he suffers because by virtue of his imprisonment he cannot travel, he cannot go to Spain, and he cannot get on with the task of taking the gospel to the ends of the earth. It is heartbreaking to him. Paul suffers because other Christians are stirring up trouble; motivated by envy and rivalry, they are criticizing Paul. While he puts a good face on it by declaring that it does not matter as long as the gospel gets preached, it has to hurt. Paul suffers over the disunity in the Philippian church, polarized by two powerful women leaders. He suffers most because he longs to be with Christ, yet it is necessary for him to be here.

Gen X resonates with Paul. His spirituality resonates with their spirituality. They understand Philippians 1:29: "For it has been granted to you on behalf of Christ not only to believe on him [here is this issue of *phronesis*], but also to suffer for him" — self-emptying sacrifice.

Let me end with a quotation from Richard Bauckham's book *Bible and Mission: Christian Witness in a Postmodern World:*

> Witness to this God is always also witness against idolatry, contending with the false witnesses to the idols who are no-gods. The projects of the idols are indeed often projections of the aspirations and frustrations of the human will to power. We should certainly think today, among others, of the greedy, never-satisfied idols that lurk behind the ideology of consumerism in its project to dominate the whole of life and the whole globe. . . . Paul confronts such projects with the cross of Christ that shows the gospel to be radically unassimilable to such projects. . . . Paul's account of the cross as the critical test of the *content* of the church's witness is also . . . an account of the cross as the critical test of the form of the church's witness. The way that, as an apostle of Christ, Paul lived and preached could serve the gospel only by not conforming to the social values and strategies that the message of the cross contradicts. . . . [T]he church's mission is inseparable from the church's community life as the living of an alternative way in contradistinction to its socio-cultural context.[6]

6. Richard Bauckham, *Bible and Mission: Christian Witness in a Postmodern World* (Grand Rapids: Baker Academic, 2003), pp. 100-103.

This is the vision of the "emerging church." This is the vision of Dr. Villafañe. May this vision prevail, and may it be sustained over time as the "emerging church" matures. It is young now, and it is just beginning to find its shape and voice. May this vision prevail as Gen X ages and begins to get its piece of the American pie. Their boomer forerunners in the Jesus movement also began churches, but, with some notable exceptions (like the missional church), these churches did not resist the culture over the long haul. So now we look at them and find "cheap grace."

So the question is: Which vision of the church will prevail in the twenty-first century? That which seems to accommodate the ideology of consumerism and the other idols of the age, or that which puts the cross at the center of its witness and its community life, as Dr. Villafañe has described in his stirring call?

"El Verbo fue Hecho Carne": The Incarnation and Theological Education

Introduction

The beginning of a new millennium is an opportune time to reflect on the challenges that we face in theological education. It is also, I believe, an opportune time to think *theologically* about theological education.

Theological education is a broad, relevant, and complex theme. And it is even more so when we underline its three major publics — that is, the church, the academy, and society.[1]

To think theologically about theological education is, among other things, to look at our present situation through the biblical-theological lenses that define our faith. And a central fact of our faith is the incarnation. As Paul

---

1. See, among others, David Tracy, "A Social Portrait of the Theologian — The Three Publics of Theology: Society, Academy and Church," in *The Analogical Imagination: Christian Thought and the Culture of Pluralism* (New York: Crossroad, 1981), pp. 3-46.

would remind us, "God was reconciling the world to himself in Christ" (2 Cor. 5:19). And in those memorable words of John, "The Word became flesh" (John 1:14). Great indeed is the mystery of Jesus, "the Word of God" (Rev. 19:13) — truly God, truly human, truly one!

The mystery and greatness of the incarnation are explored by Miguel De Unamuno in one of my favorite poetic works, *El Cristo de Velázquez*, which has been said by many to be one of the greatest treatises on the incarnation. "Listen" and "see" the poetic and theological truth in the following brief verses, first in Spanish:

> . . . para ver tu cuerpo blanco que en desnudez al Padre retrataba desnudo. Destapaste a nuestros ojos la humanidad de Dios; Con tus dos brazos desabrochando el manto del misterio, nos revelaste la divina esencia, la humanidad de Dios, la que el hombre descubre lo divino.

And now in English:

> . . . to see your white body that in nakedness the Father you pictured naked. You uncovered to our eyes the humanity of God; with your two arms unbuttoning the mantle of mystery, you revealed to us the divine essence, the humanity of God, by which man discovers the divine.[2]

2. Miguel De Unamuno, *El Cristo de Velázquez* (Poema) (Madrid: Esposa-Calpe, 1967), p. 24; the translation from the Spanish is my own.

For Unamuno, the incarnation reveals the humanity of God, and in so doing it affirms unequivocally the value and the goodness of creation. Christianity does not reject the world — creation, humanity, and its culture. Rather, Christianity can comprehend its God in Jesus Christ only through the world. Unamuno teaches us this profound truth about our knowledge of God being understood only *by* and *through* the incarnation. His *El Cristo de Velázquez* is an expression of and commentary on the Scripture verse in his book's epigraph, which Unamuno quotes in Greek: *kai ho kurio to somati* ("and the Lord for the body," 1 Cor. 6:13).

I agree with the following statement by church historian Justo González:

> I continue to be convinced that the focal point of all Christian theology that merits such a name is the Incarnation of God in Jesus Christ. This does not mean methodologically that all theology must begin with Christology. It is possible to begin with the Trinitarian doctrine (Barth, Bonaventure), with the unity of God (Thomas Aquinas), with the experience of grace (Luther), with the doctrine of man (Reinhold Niebuhr), with the experience of dependence (Schleiermacher), etc., etc. But always, in all these cases and in any other, the focal point by which one must judge all theology is how it understands that "God was in Christ reconciling the world to himself."[3]

3. Justo González, "Encarnación e Historia," in *Fe Cristiana y Latino-*

My intent in this essay is to underline the importance of the incarnation as a frame of reference for our theological education — in other words, to underline that the focal point by which all theological education is to be judged is, explicitly or implicitly, how it understands the incarnation. My principal thesis is simple, and it can be summarized in the following manner: The incarnation as a reality, symbol, or principle should inform the mission and task of theological education and, thus, the relationship that theological education has with the church, the academy, and the society.

The limits of this essay do not permit a detailed analysis or elaboration of the tremendous truth of the incarnation and the multiple ways in which it informs theological education. Nevertheless, I want to share briefly and provisionally some lessons and truths that I have learned and that I believe are pertinent. First I want to make some observations about the incarnation and the mission of theological education. Then I want to share with you a christological typology and briefly discuss how this typology informs the task of theological education.

---

américa Hoy, ed. C. René Padilla (Buenos Aires: Ediciones Certeza, 1974), pp. 154-55. Among the many works on the incarnation, see the classic by St. Athanasius, *On the Incarnation: The Treatise De Incarnatione Verbi Dei* (Crestwood, NY: St. Vladimir's Seminary Press, 2000); for a modern and provocative work on the biblical concept of incarnation, see Jon L. Berquist, *Incarnation* (St. Louis: Chalice Press, 1999); for a work on "incarnational mission," see Darrell L. Guder, *The Incarnation and the Church's Witness* (Harrisburg, PA: Trinity Press International, 1999).

The Incarnation and the Mission
of Theological Education

The issues involved in the mission of theological education are many and varied. One can address the mission of theological education by underlining a particular set of issues or themes. Two such themes that I want to emphasize here are globalization and contextualization. For at the heart of a theology of the incarnation is the understanding that the incarnation is the expression par excellence of the global and contextual love of God, a global and contextual love that should also define the mission of theological education.[4]

A global and contextual love highlights the mission of a compassionate God whose love knows no boundary. In 2 Corinthians 5:19, Paul tells us that "God was reconciling the world to himself in Christ." And in the well-known and profound words of John 3:16: "For God so loved the world that he gave his one and only Son, that whoever believes in him shall not perish but have eternal life." For God so loved the WORLD!

Globalization is a popular word today. It means different things to different people. While we are all familiar with the ubiquitous number-crunching of the global market, for theological education globalization means something else. Let me outline for you, briefly, at least six different empha-

4. In this section on globalization and contextualization, I draw upon my essay, "A Prayer for the City: Paul's Benediction and a Vision for Urban Theological Education," in my book, *A Prayer for the City: Further Reflections on Urban Ministry* (Austin, TX: AETH, 2001), pp. 3-16.

ses and perspectives on globalization that should inform the mission of theological education:

1. the emphasis on globalization as evangelization: this means the great challenge of sharing by word and deed the gospel of our Lord Jesus Christ and his reign, and making disciples of all nations;
2. the focus on globalization as *shalom:* this means seeking the peace of the city (cf. Jer. 29:7) — that is, the wholeness, welfare, prosperity, health, reconciliation, liberation, justice, and salvation of the cities of the world;
3. the emphasis on globalization as social justice or human development: this means seeking to improve the welfare of suffering people in the city and around the world;
4. the focus on globalization as ecumenism: this means encouraging greater cooperation and understanding among churches and people with different Christian theologies in our cities;
5. the stress on globalization as interreligious dialogue: this means communicating and bridging the gaps, where possible, between the world's major religions in our pluralistic urban world;
6. the accent on globalization as cultural, gender, and racial equity and diversity: this means the appreciation, affirmation, and appropriation of the multicultural, multiracial, and feminist (or "mujerista") contribution in all human endeavors.[5]

5. See Donald E. Messer, *Calling Church and Seminary into the*

The global love of God compels us to embrace in the mission of theological education the breadth of these multiple meanings and perspectives of globalization.

Donald E. Messer, former president of the Iliff School of Theology, notes in his book *Calling Church and Seminary into the Twenty-First Century* that "it is a global or universal love that we must teach and preach. It is the love of Christ that transcends every barrier, every nation, every race, every culture, and every people. . . . It is the love of God and neighbor that underlies our reason for being in the business of theological education."[6]

But this "global love" needs to be contextualized in our urban world — thus my special concern for urban theological education. In that well-known hymn found in Philippians 2 we read:

> Your attitude should be the same as that
>   of Christ Jesus:
> Who, being in very nature God,
>   did not consider equality with God something
>   to be grasped,
> but made himself nothing,
>   taking the very nature of a servant,
>   being made in human likeness.

Twenty-First Century (Nashville: Abingdon Press, 1995), p. 57. The first, third, fourth, and fifth perspectives represent Don S. Browning's contribution, and the second and sixth perspectives are my emphasis.

6. Messer, *Calling Church and Seminary into the Twenty-First Century*, p. 57.

And being found in appearance as a man,
 he humbled himself
 and became obedient to death — even death
  on a cross!

(Phil. 2:5-8)

Here we have a record of God's incarnated and redemptive love in the person of his son Jesus Christ ("the Word became flesh"). In this passage, Paul notes the self-emptying *(kenosis)* of Christ and his final humiliation on the cross. This is a very important theological passage that not only speaks about the incarnation per se but also has been a source of great insight for developing strategic models of redemptive theological education and urban ministry.

This passage speaks to us of one who became human and lived among us. And as the Gospels make clear, it speaks of one who in his life and work identified himself with the marginalized, the downtrodden, and the poor — as Paul would say in his first letter to the Corinthians, "the foolish things of the world . . . the weak things of the world . . . the lowly things of this world" (1 Cor. 1:27-28). What is my point here? It's simple. Theological education must continually be reminded to humbly express an "urban *kenosis*." That is, it must empty itself of the prerogatives of power and prestige, so highly valued by academia and the world, and pitch its tent among the poor and marginalized communities in our cities.

While theological education seeks to serve the whole city — the neighborhood as well as the greater metropolitan area — it begins with and contextually expresses a commitment to and solidarity with those whom the Master did. In the language of Leonardo Boff or Gustavo Gutiérrez, it must manifest "a preferential option for the poor."

Karl Barth stated it well: "God always takes his stand unconditionally and passionately on this side and this side alone: against the lofty and on behalf of the lowly, against those who enjoy right and privilege and on behalf of those who are denied it and deprived of it."[7] And again he said, in another context: "The Church is witness of the fact that the Son of God came to seek and save the lost. And this implies that — casting all false impartiality aside — the Church must concentrate first on the lower and lowest levels of human society. The poor, the socially and economically weak and threatened, will always be the object of its primary and particular concern."[8]

One of the many challenges that confront the urban churches today is the need for trained leadership — not just more clergy, but grass-roots leadership, women and men, who are both called by God and empowered by the Spirit to make a difference in their communities. Theological education that is geared to training the indigenous leadership of urban churches in the context of their everyday ministry is needed on all levels. Unfortunately, much of theological education does not critically fit the urban scene, often choos-

7. Karl Barth, *Church Dogmatics*, ed. T. F. Torrance and Geoffrey W. Bromiley (Edinburgh: T. & T. Clark, 1956-1975), II/1, p. 386.

8. Karl Barth, "The Christian Community and the Civil Community," in *Against the Stream* (London: SCM Press, 1934), p. 36.

ing to ignore the city as a positive locus of God's redemptive activity. The result is an educational process and product that approach urban ministry as a problem to be solved rather than as an opportunity to discover the signs of God's reign. Thus, many institutions and programs are not contextualized to the urban environment; do not take into account the experience, gifts, and expertise of the existing leadership; and are not reflective of the communities that are in the city. Their educational policies, curriculum, and teaching methodologies do not "fit" a diverse constituency. The community has no "ownership" of the program and thus participates to a marginal degree.

In contrast, the Center for Urban Ministerial Education (CUME) of Gordon-Conwell Theological Seminary in Boston has grappled with these realities. Undergirding all of CUME's educational philosophy and structure, from the diploma to the doctoral programs, is the concept of contextualized urban theological education. In this way, CUME has structured itself to be *in* the city, *of* the city, and *for* and *with* the city.

Contextualization (or incarnation) is the *sine qua non* ("without which not") of all faithful and effective urban theological education. In reflecting on the mission of theological education, my prayer is that we would understand that theological education can do no less than the breadth (globalization) and depth (contextualization) to which the incarnational love of God points us.

A Christological Typology

The mystery of the incarnation is unfathomable. The history of Christian thought reveals the grueling battles of the early church. In it we see the church's struggles with distinct factions and often extreme positions regarding the incarnation. These were "extreme positions which appeared to contradict the central message of the Gospel that 'God was in Christ.'"[9] Furthermore, these christological battles of the early centuries were brutal, and not always because of the theological complexities of the issues, but rather due to the "strong hand" of the ecclesiastical and political powers.

There are essentially six heresies regarding the person of Christ, all of which appeared within the first four Christian centuries, and which, sad to say, reappear now and then throughout church history. These heresies can be presented in three distinct pairs, pairs that respond to the question of the deity, humanity, and unity of Jesus Christ.

> The first pair: the heresies that deny the genuineness (Ebionism) or the completeness (Arianism) of the *deity* of Jesus.
>
> The second pair: the heresies that deny the genuineness (Docetism) or the completeness (Apollinarianism) of the *humanity* of Jesus.
>
> The third pair: the heresies that, in response to the *unity*

9. González, "Encarnación e Historia," p. 155. Throughout this essay, and particularly in this section, I am indebted to the inspiration of Justo González in his insightful essay.

of Jesus, divided his person (Nestorianism) or confused his nature (Monophysitism).[10]

I will begin by briefly defining the three pairs of the typology, without going deeply or thoroughly into the theological thought of its protagonists or advocates. I will also make some comments on the "Definition of Faith" of the Council of Chalcedon (A.D. 451) as a corrective response.

The Deity of Jesus Christ

Our first pair of heresies are those that denied the genuineness or the completeness of the deity of Jesus Christ. Here we note that some persons affirmed the human reality of Jesus Christ but denied God's presence in him. That is, the *genuineness* of the deity of Jesus was questioned by the Ebionites. For them, "the distance between God and

10. See Millard J. Erickson, *Christian Theology*, 2nd ed. (Grand Rapids: Baker Books, 1999), p. 755; Justo González, "And the Word Was Made Flesh," in *Mañana: Christian Theology from a Hispanic Perspective* (Nashville: Abingdon, 1990), pp. 139-55; González, "The Christological Debates to the Council of Chalcedon," in his *The Story of Christianity: The Early Church to the Dawn of the Reformation*, vol. 1 (New York: Harper & Row, 1984), pp. 252-57; and especially chapters 16-17 in González, *A History of Christian Thought: From the Beginnings to the Council of Chalcedon*, vol. 1, rev. ed. (Nashville: Abingdon, 1987), pp. 335-80; see also Jon Sobrino, "La Cristología Conciliar," in *La Fe en Jesucristo: Ensayo desde las víctimas* (Madrid: Editorial Trotta, 1999), pp. 315-464; and Luis Pedraja, *Jesus Is My Uncle: Christology from a Hispanic Perspective* (Nashville: Abingdon, 1999).

the world is uncrossable and all attempts to see God in the world are idolatry."[11]

There were also those who denied the *completeness* of the deity of Jesus: the Arians. In their interest to safeguard the absolute uniqueness and transcendence of God, the Arians denied the completeness (or integrity) of the deity of Jesus. For them Jesus Christ was not the eternal Word, but only a perfect being — and a created one at that — and therefore not God with a capital "G."

The Humanity of Jesus Christ

Our second pair of heresies are those that denied the genuineness or the completeness of the humanity of Jesus Christ. Some persons affirmed the presence of God (deity) in Jesus Christ, but denied the reality (or *genuineness*) of his human existence. These, the Docetists, viewed matter as evil, and so to them the appearance of Jesus Christ was just that — human appearance, not a reality. For them "God is a spiritual being that has nothing to do with this physical world."[12]

Others denied the *completeness* of the humanity of Jesus Christ. Here we find the followers of Apollinarius. In the interest of safeguarding the unity of the deity and humanity of Christ, Apollinarius affirmed the humanity in the body of Jesus, but denied the existence of a human rational soul in

11. González, "Encarnación e Historia," p. 156.
12. González, "Encarnación e Historia," p. 155.

him. In other words, "Jesus was human physically, but not psychologically. He had a human body, but not a human soul. His soul was divine."[13] Thus, such a view denied the completeness (integrity) of the humanity of Jesus Christ.

The Unity of Jesus Christ

The final pair of heresies, the third pair in the typology, have to do with the unity of Jesus Christ. The issue in question is how the human and divine unite in Jesus Christ, or what is the relationship between the two natures. Here we note that there were those who divided the person of Jesus Christ and others who confused his nature.

Nestorianism represented the school of thought that presented a clear *division* between the human and the divine in Jesus Christ. For example, the miracles of Jesus were attributed to his divinity; but if Jesus was thirsty or hungry, that feeling was attributed to his humanity. The Nestorians' position "for all intents and purposes dissolved the Incarnation into two realities that never come to unite."[14]

Others took an opposite position from Nestorianism. These, the followers of Eutyches, taught what was known as monophysitism — that is, the doctrine of the "one nature." For monophysitism, the deity and humanity of Jesus are united in such a way that the distinction does not exist —

13. Erickson, *Christian Theology*, p. 731.
14. González, "Encarnación e Historia," p. 157.

they are *confused*. In such a case the humanity of Jesus is lost in his divinity.

The Council of Chalcedon

At the Council of Chalcedon (A.D. 451), the church was finally able to achieve a "definition of faith" that affirmed the full divinity as well as the full humanity of Jesus, while affirming the unity of Christ without division or confusion. Thus, it is in the "definition of faith" of Chalcedon that the church establishes the parameters that have been considered christologically orthodox.

Referring to the resolutions of both the Council of Nicea (A.D. 325) and the Council of Chalcedon (A.D. 451), Gabriel Fackre asks:

> Who is Jesus Christ? He is *truly God, truly human, truly one*. This fundamental doctrine of the Incarnation — Deity, humanity, and unity of Jesus Christ — is the Church's effort to be faithful to the figure it met and meets in the pages of the Bible and in its own life with him.[15]

The significance of Chalcedon goes beyond the importance of resolving the theological issue of Christ's nature.

15. Gabriel Fackre, *The Christian Story: A Narrative Interpretation of Basic Christian Doctrine* (Grand Rapids: Eerdmans, 1984), p. 99 (Fackre's emphasis).

Ultimately, it is critical to a proper understanding of Jesus' life and mission, and to a proper affirmation of humanity and history.

The Christological Typology and Theological Education

Let me now make some brief remarks on how this very suggestive christological typology informs the task of theological education. In it we have noted three pairs that respond to the question of the *deity, humanity,* and *unity* of Jesus Christ.

One of the major problems that we find in our churches and schools (be they Bible institutes, colleges, or seminaries) is their tendency toward Docetism. Such a Docetism takes many forms, but it shows itself in a curriculum that tends to overemphasize the so-called spiritual (or the nonmaterial) over the physical or human. In this case, the so-called spiritual lacks a proper biblical understanding of the integrity of the human person and of a "spirituality" defined by the presence of the Holy Spirit in creation.

In the pertinent words of Justo González:

> Nature, in the sense of the created cosmos, is the work of God — indeed, in that sense nature is a spiritual creation, for Genesis 1:2 says that "the Spirit of God was moving over the face of the waters."
>
> All things that God has made, God has made

44

through the Spirit. All things that God now does, God does through the Spirit. All things that God will do, God will do through the Spirit. In this sense, all created reality is the result of the work of the Spirit and has a spiritual dimension.[16]

The danger of Docetism in the curriculum is that it tends to deny our sense of belonging or relationship with the created world. There is a critical need for a biblical "re-enchantment" of our natural world. A proper stewardship of our human and natural ecological reality demands it. In other words, we must recapture a holistic sense of spirituality — one that goes beyond a sterile dualism, affirms the created world, and for that reason takes spiritual responsibility for it; one that reflects the Lordship over all creation of the "Word made flesh."

In many other churches and schools, theological education has tended to fall into an implicit Ebionism, and a potentially dangerous one at that. In this case the Ebionism displayed tends to emphasize and value the human and human action so much that it has devalued ever so subtly the divine dimension. Here we see the propensity of a theological education for what I call a "reductionism to the human" — that is, reducing the purpose, goal, and meaning of the religious life to "human" fulfillment and value.

In its "liberal" manifestation, we see teaching that is so committed to human progress and so-called human rights

16. González, *Mañana*, p. 160.

and justice that the divine or "spiritual" dimension of life is practically denied.

In "conservative" circles, the manifestation of Ebionism is to be found in the teachings of that enticing message of "health and wealth." One cannot watch a religious television program without sooner or later confronting a "prosperity gospel" message. Too many churches and schools, however biblically they portray themselves, are toying with this ultimately Ebionistic theology in their pulpits and curriculum.

One of the perennial debates in theological education concerns preserving the unity or integration of the curriculum.[17] This debate has taken many forms and followed many currents; for example, the theory-practice split divides the curriculum into two camps — the theoretical or academic and the practical or ministerial. Such a split tends toward "Nestorianism," inasmuch as it recognizes both disciplines (or camps), but in its desire to preserve the given curriculum it votes in favor of a division (of the disciplines or camps) that never becomes united.

17. Among the many recent works dealing with this and other pertinent issues in theological education, see Edward Farley, *Theologia: The Fragmentation and Unity of Theological Education* (Philadelphia: Fortress, 1983); David Kelsey, *Between Athens and Berlin: The Theological Education Debate* (Philadelphia: Fortress, 1983); Robert Banks, *Reenvisioning Theological Education: Exploring a Missional Alternative to Current Models* (Grand Rapids: Eerdmans, 1999); Eldin Villafañe, Bruce W. Jackson, Robert A. Evans, and Alice Frazer Evans, *Transforming the City: Reframing Education for Urban Ministry* (Grand Rapids: Eerdmans, 2002); and Roberto Pazmiño, *Foundational Issues in Christian Education: An Introduction in Evangelical Perspective* (Grand Rapids: Baker Book House, 1988).

Implicitly, this is a position that philosophically, as well as pedagogically, separates reflection from action, and action from reflection. In reality, given the power plays and prestige in our theological institutions, this position results in the dominance or hegemony of the so-called theoretical over the practical — in itself an "intellectual Docetism."

Occasionally in some of our schools — and, sad to say, very often in many of our churches — one finds the opposite. In these cases, a not very subtle anti-intellectual emphasis results in a false unity where, in reality, the practical or activist has dominance or hegemony — in itself a "pragmatic Ebionism."

Every effort to unite or integrate the disciplines of study or the curriculum must remember the "body-soul" or "mind-body" unity of the human person. Therefore, a wise resolution, informed by the "definition of faith" of Chalcedon, will attempt to keep reflection (or the intellectual) and action (or the practical) in a dynamic dialectic in which both sides mutually inform each other — without division or confusion. In the best case scenario, this dialectic would involve reflection *in* as well as reflection *on* ministry and life.

Those responsible for theological education, whether at the church, school, or seminary, must wrestle with those biblical paradigms that undergird the action/reflection methodology. That means that we must take another look at the leadership models of Samuel and the school of prophets, Jesus and the disciples, and Paul and the school of

Tyrannus (Acts 19) — all missional models, by the way — to inform our curriculum.[18]

Conclusion

The incarnation has many lessons for theological education. In many and diverse ways, the church, the academy, and society cry out for critical theological reflection by all who, by the grace of God, have stewardship over theological education. Serious reflection on the incarnation, I believe, will help us to be faithful to that stewardship — that is, if we permit the incarnation to inform our global and contextual mission and if we permit it to inform the task of theological education.

Let me close with an extended quote by Karl Barth, from his essay "The Humanity of God":

> Jesus Christ is in His one Person, as true *God, man's* loyal partner, and as true *man, God's.* He is the Lord humbled for communion with man and likewise the Servant exalted to communion with God. He is the Word spoken from the loftiest, most luminous transcendence and likewise the Word heard in the deepest, darkest immanence. He is both, without their being confused but also without their being divided;

18. See Banks, *Reenvisioning Theological Education,* especially pp. 71-126.

He is wholly the one and wholly the other. Thus in this oneness Jesus Christ is the Mediator, the Reconciler, between God and man. Thus He comes forward to *man* on behalf of *God* calling for and awakening faith, love, and hope, and to *God* on behalf of *man,* representing man, making satisfaction and interceding. Thus He attests and guarantees to man God's free *grace* and at the same time attests and guarantees to God man's free *gratitude.* Thus He establishes in His Person the justice of God vis-à-vis man and also the justice of man before God. Thus He is in His Person the covenant in its fullness, the Kingdom of heaven which is at hand, in which God speaks and man hears, God gives and man receives, God commands and man obeys, God's glory shines in the heights and thence into the depths, and peace on earth comes to pass among men in whom He is well pleased. Moreover, exactly in this way Jesus Christ, as this Mediator and Reconciler between God and man, is also the *Revealer* of them both. We do not need to engage in a free-ranging investigation to seek out and construct who and what God truly is, and who and what man truly is, but only to read the truth about both where it resides, namely, in the fullness of their togetherness, their covenant which proclaims itself in Jesus Christ.[19]

19. Karl Barth, *The Humanity of God* (Atlanta: John Knox Press, 1976), pp. 46-47 (Barth's emphasis).

"'El Verbo fue Hecho Carne'"

Juan Francisco Martinez

Dr. Villafañe, thank you very much for your challenge to us to think theologically about theological education. By using the analogies of incarnation and the nature of Christ, you provide the seminary with important resources for its task.

I want to respond at several levels. First of all, I want to make a couple of general comments. Then I want to think about the two major theological themes addressed by Dr. Villafañe and their implications for our task here at Fuller Seminary. My hope is to point in some possible directions for the future.

First my general comments. To begin with, thank you for beginning your lecture with a quote from Miguel De Unamuno. It is not often that someone who wrote primarily in Spanish is considered of sufficient depth to merit being used as a reference point for theological reflection.

A second general comment has to do with the title of your lecture. You chose to use the Spanish quote from John

1:14. Since you did that, I was expecting some comment about how *logos* has been translated into English and into Spanish. The Guatemalan pop singer Ricardo Arjona says in one of his most popular songs that God is a verb, not a noun *(Dios es verbo, no sustantivo)*. What are the theological implications of translating *logos* into "Verb," instead of "Word," as in most English translations of the Bible? What are the dynamic vs. static implications of each translation, and how does each affect the way we understand the incarnation and our task in theological education?

After those general comments, I would now like to focus on the core of the lecture. There is no doubt that the incarnation is an indispensable frame of reference for us as Christians. We cannot develop a Christian theology or understand God's work in the world apart from the incarnation. If the church cannot understand its mission without the framework of the incarnation, then theological educators cannot prepare "men and women for the manifold ministries of Christ and his church" without a clear understanding of the incarnation.

In this section, Dr. Villafañe chooses to focus on two emphases that are crucial to the mission of the church: globalization and contextualization. In other words, the incarnation must manifest itself in the urban reality created by sinful humanity. This puts the church in the United States in a difficult spot. On the one hand, we are forced to struggle with Jacques Ellul and others to come up with a theological understanding of the city. Scripture begins in a garden, and the city usually represents the worst of human attempts to develop a society that does not need God. Yet Scripture looks forward to a city. The theological tension is easily illustrated in popular culture, where the sci-fi question is whether to look forward to the Babylon 5 of *Star Trek* or the Zion of *Matrix* fame. One is clearly a human creation; the other depends on the death of a savior. So is the city a sign of human rebellion or a place that can be redeemed as part of God's re-creation?

Yet the principal problem with the city is not the theological ambivalence but the very practical fact that American evangelicalism is a church of the suburbs. Evangelicals have fled the city and have developed a comfortable lifestyle in the suburbs. Our churches are structured for the suburb and are most effective in that context.

And this affects seminary education. Recently at Fuller, we were having a discussion related to the Hispanic Church Studies M.Div. concentration. The implication seemed to be that the Hispanic M.Div. was ethnically specific, but the English language M.Div. was for all. Yet one of my colleagues quickly clarified this when he said that if there were truth in advertising, one would have to say that the general Fuller M.Div. is really a white, suburban, middle-class M.Div. Upon completing an M.Div. at Fuller one is most qualified to be an associate pastor at an evangelical suburban mega-church, according to my colleague.

The problem is also practical for a place like Fuller that is tuition driven. Between storefront churches and suburban mega-churches, which is the seminary's primary audi-

ence? Which pays the bills? But if Jesus loves the city, does
he love suburbanites too?

Fuller is also having to address this issue in relationship to the Association of Theological Schools (ATS) and
the Western Association of Schools and Colleges (WASC).
The academy has a certain standard and model. Students
need to have sufficient education to fit into a university
model of training for ministry. But most world cities are not
sending their best and future leaders to universities. Where
do inner-city Bible institutes fit in the equation? So how
does Fuller serve the city? To use Dr. Villafañe's term, what
does "urban *kenosis*" mean for Fuller? How does Fuller en-
ter the city, and how does the city become a co-owner of
Fuller's task? How does our seminary demonstrate a "preferential option for the poor"?

I would like to suggest some tentative ways that we at
Fuller can point to as we take Dr. Villafañe's challenge seriously. Using the incarnation as the reference point, here are
some ideas that can help us in our task of preparing women
and men to serve in the increasingly urban world.

First of all, we need to recognize the incarnation as *theological method*. This means that all theology is contextual
and needs to be contextualized if it is to respond to the questions of our urban world. Fuller is working very hard in this
area. But there is still a bit of a sense that our theological reflection has to be referenced in light of the work of a number of dead European males. Without denying the value of
those theologies, we need to recognize that the work of St.
Barth was just as contextualized as liberation, feminist, or

Latino theologies. They are all attempts to incarnate and explain God's work in the world in light of specific contextual situations.

Second, the incarnation needs to serve as a *hermeneutical method*. We need to give our students tools to exegete Scripture in and for the city, but also to exegete the city in light of the Scripture. Our students need tools to interpret the multiethnic complexities of Los Angeles and other cities in light of God's work in the world.

The incarnation also needs to help us in a third area, *practical theology*. We need to teach and model ministry as incarnation. Many of our students are already involved in the life of the city. Our task is to give them tools to help them become Christ to the city — no small challenge.

Dr. Villafañe's second major point relates to Christology. He states that seminaries have been guilty of one christological heresy or another. There are no major surprises here. Our students come from churches where these heresies are lived out, and we are also a reflection of those same churches. As an Anabaptist, I have always known that I am a heretic (after all, Calvin told me so). So Dr. Villafañe's analysis is a comforting thought. But his challenge carries serious implications for us. How do we keep in tension the various aspects of our task without subsuming one to the others? What does a "dynamic dialectic" look like at Fuller?

Dean Howard Loewen recently asked Art Patzia, Jim Butler, and me to attend a Carnegie Foundation seminar on clergy education. Carnegie has been involved in a major study of how professional schools train students for the professions, including the clergy. And though their report was couched in a different analogy, they basically found that most seminaries in the United States and Canada suffer from, to use Dr. Villafañe's analogy, a form of Nestorianism. On the one hand, there is the separation of the guilds and a subsequent prioritizing, with theology and Bible as the queens, practical ministry as a tolerated second cousin, and the rest somewhere in between. But the Carnegie study also implies that there is a Nestorianism related to the various tasks a seminary needs to accomplish to adequately prepare people to be effective in the parish.

Bill Sullivan, one of the major presenters at the Carnegie seminar, spoke of three apprenticeships that need to be developed in a professional school so that a student can be effective in her chosen profession. According to Sullivan, students preparing for ministry (or any other profession) need to be apprenticed in three areas: (1) intellectual, cognitive learning; (2) a body of skills; and (3) the values of the professional group. (This sounds very much like the "know, be, do" triad that some have advocated for Fuller's Expanded Course Descriptions [ECDs].) According to the initial results of the Carnegie study, professional institutions, including seminaries, are very good at the first, give some focus to the second, but do not deal with the third.

These triads challenge us to recognize not only the importance of each but also the need for that "dynamic dialectic." Western education has done a very good job of separating out each part and defining it carefully. We have departments to deal with some of the apprenticeships. But where does Fuller help students deal with the values, and where do we give them tools to put all they are learning into some kind of coherent whole? Whether we use words like "integration" or "dynamic dialectic," the challenge is crucial.

If this were not confusing enough, our christological conundrum has to do with holding the human and the divine in dialectic tension. We do not want to subsume, mix, or confuse the two natures of Christ. In terms of our task, the question is: where does the Holy Spirit fit in all of this? This query reminds us that we constantly have to return humbly to the fact that our task is always limited, only a small part of what God is doing in and through us.

Dr. Villafañe suggests that we need to go to the past if we are to find models to guide us into the future. Yet here he challenges us again. How does a mega-seminary take small group discipleship models seriously?

Thank you for your challenge to us, Dr. Villafañe. You have given us plenty of grist. Our mills will be working overtime for a long time.

Amos, Intrepid Leader for Justice: Three Indispensable Qualities of a Minister of the Word of God

10 *Then Amaziah the priest of Bethel sent a message to King Jeroboam of Israel: "Amos is raising a conspiracy against you in the very heart of Israel. The land cannot bear all his words.* 11 *For this is what Amos is saying: 'Jeroboam will die by the sword, and Israel will surely go into exile, away from their native land.'"* 12 *Then Amaziah said to Amos, "Get out, you seer! Go back to the land of Judah. Earn your bread there and do your prophesying there.* 13 *Don't prophesy anymore at Bethel, because this is the king's sanctuary and the temple of the kingdom."* 14 *Amos answered Amaziah, "I was neither a prophet nor a prophet's son, but I was a shepherd, and I also took care of sycamore-fig trees.* 15 *But the LORD took me from tending the flock and said to me, 'Go, prophesy to my people Israel.'"*

AMOS 7:10-15

57

Introduction

Lately I have been reading about the great reformer Martin Luther. Few figures in church history have so revolutionized the face of Christendom. In reading much or even a little of the life of Martin Luther, one cannot help but be challenged and inspired by the courageous stance of this intrepid leader. For as we know, then as now, a leader's character is revealed when it is put to the test — when it is under pressure!

You all know the scenario well. It was April 18, 1521. Luther had been called to Worms to appear before the emperor, the court, and the church examiner, John Eck. He was to give account for his writings. Roland Bainton depicts the central dialogue graphically in his book, *Here I Stand: A Life of Martin Luther:*

> "I ask you, Martin — answer cordially and without horns — do you or do you not repudiate your books and the errors which they contain?"
>
> Luther replied, "Since then your Majesty and your Lordship desire a simple reply, I will answer without horns and without teeth. Unless I am convicted by Scripture and plain reason — I do not accept the authority of popes and councils, for they have contradicted each other — my conscience is captive to the Word of God. I cannot and I will not recant anything, for to go against conscience is neither

right nor safe. Here I stand, I cannot do otherwise. God help me. Amen."[1]

Martin Luther was indeed an intrepid leader. He challenged the political and ecclesiastical power of the empire. Many have asked through the ages, what kind of man is this? What kind of leader is he? As we look through the pages of history, we are not surprised to find many Christian leaders — men and women — to whom can be applied the words of the writer of the book of Hebrews: "who through faith conquered kingdoms, administered justice, and gained what was promised; who shut the mouths of lions, quenched the fury of the flames, and escaped the edge of the sword; whose weakness was turned to strength; and who became powerful in battle and routed foreign armies" (Heb. 11:33-34). These were, and still are, men and women of God, men and women obsessed and possessed by God and God's Word. We live in times that demand intrepid, courageous leaders, men and women of God ready to proclaim by word and deed the truth, the holiness, and the justice of God!

In the biblical passage cited above from Amos 7, we are faced with an autobiographical scenario not unlike the one faced by Martin Luther at the Diet of Worms. In this biblical passage, we find the king's chaplain — the priest Amaziah — confronting God's chosen leader, the prophet

---

1. Roland H. Bainton, *Here I Stand: A Life of Martin Luther* (New York: Abingdon, 1950), p. 144.

Amos.[2] We also find in the prophet Amos at least three indispensable qualities of a minister of the Word of God:

1. a strong sense of God's calling;
2. a sure word from God;
3. singular courage from God.

The world in which we live is crying out for leaders with these qualities. There are many issues, causes, and challenges in our present world that you and I must confront if we are to be true to the gospel of our Lord Jesus Christ, and we must face these challenges with the same leadership qualities as Amos.

A Strong Sense of God's Calling

Amos, a Man Called of God

Amos was a leader with a strong sense of God's calling. Note the words of Amos 7:14-15:

2. Among the many and excellent texts on the book of Amos, see Mark Daniel Carroll R., *Contexts for Amos: Prophetic Poetics in Latin American Perspective* (Sheffield: Sheffield Academic Press, 1992); James L. Mays, *Amos: A Commentary* (Philadelphia: Westminster, 1969); Douglas Stuart, *Hosea-Jonah*, Word Biblical Commentary 31 (Waco: Word, 1987); Washington Padilla, *Amós-Abdías*, Comentario Biblico Hispanoamericano (Miami: Editorial Caribe, 1989); and Hans W. Wolff, *Joel and Amos*, Hermeneia (Philadelphia: Fortress, 1977).

Amos answered Amaziah, "I was neither a prophet nor a prophet's son, but I was a shepherd, and I also took care of sycamore-fig trees. But the LORD took me from tending the flock and said to me, 'Go, prophesy to my people Israel.'"

Amos was not brought up in the class from which prophets usually came. He was not trained for the prophethood in the prophetic schools or guilds. Amos was simply a layperson.

One cannot help but wonder about the spiritual state of the professional clergy at this time. There must have been other prophets or priests in the land — learned clergy, I'm sure, who were no doubt profoundly knowledgeable about Scripture. Yet it pleased God to call this humble shepherd and cultivator of fig trees to deliver his message. History is replete with leaders outside the clergy who have been God's instruments to impact society and to further God's kingdom. The truth of the matter is that only as the hearts of all God's people, clergy and laity, are open to God's calling, to be God's witnesses in whatever vocation or ministry they may be placed, will the gospel of our Lord Jesus Christ be a transforming power to a broken world.

Amos was called from the insignificant town of Tekoa, in the Southern Kingdom (about ten miles south of Jerusalem). He was sent to Bethel in the Northern Kingdom. There Amos began his prophetic ministry during the reign of King Jeroboam II, in the eighth century B.C. This was a time of great economic prosperity. Yet in spite of their material success, the Israelites failed miserably in their relationship with God. Idolatry and injustice were rampant in the land. Though many Israelites were rich, many others were extremely poor. Worse, the rich thoughtlessly oppressed the poor.

Notwithstanding certain debate about the socioeconomic status of Amos by certain biblical scholars, I believe Amos was of the poor class himself. The depth of his empathy and his sharp analysis of poverty and oppression reflected an experience attuned to that reality. He needed two jobs to make ends meet, didn't he?

Calling and the "Development of the Soul"

I believe Amos's sense of God's calling was very much tied up with his solidarity with the poor. His self-identity was wrought in the experience of poverty, an experience that permitted him to see better what we call in Spanish "La Realidad." Amos was a ready candidate to hear the word of the Lord as God called him to be God's prophet. The calling and the message resonated with who Amos was, with a self-identity that had cultivated what Aleksandr Solzhenitsyn called "the development of the soul."[3]

Poverty, oppression, and affliction — whether physical or mental — can be an instrument that God uses to help us catch a perspective of God's character, the gospel, and even

3. Aleksandr I. Solzhenitsyn, *The Gulag Archipelago 1918-1956* (New York: Harper Collins, 1985), p. 311.

God's calling in our lives. I have had my share of experiences among the poor. I have lived among them. I work with them. I was raised in the South Bronx. Though I am not necessarily proud of having lived in the South Bronx — of experiencing and seeing poverty and oppression firsthand — I too say of the South Bronx what Solzhenitsyn said of his ten years in a wretched Soviet gulag: "Bless you, prison, for having been in my life."[4] I can say, "Bless you, South Bronx, for having been in my life." I do not glorify poverty — there is no intrinsic value in being poor. I have never met a poor person who wanted to be poor! Yet often those who have nothing or barely nothing of the necessities of life find that this experience does not permit them to cling to or be seduced by position, possessions, or power.

Solzhenitsyn wrote in his memoirs that in prison he learned that "the meaning of earthly existence lies not, as we have grown used to thinking, in prospering, but in the development of the soul."[5] And as Charles Colson later said, "It was prison that God used to restore the Nobel Laureate's Christian faith, and prison that shapes his prophetic words to Western society."

A sense of God's clear calling to you and to me for service in these critical times in which we live will be determined to a large extent by the degree to which our self-identity has been forged by whatever instrument God chooses, to bring about this "development of the soul." In

4. Solzhenitsyn, *The Gulag Archipelago*, p. 313.
5. Solzhenitsyn, *The Gulag Archipelago*, pp. 310-11.

God's sovereignty God calls you and me as God chooses, but God chooses those who are ready to hear God's call. There is a great mystery in God's calling to you and me. Yet we are, all of us, called to be God's faithful witnesses wherever and in whatever endeavor of leadership God places us.

A Sure Word from God

Amos was a leader with a sure word from God. If we look at Amos 7 (or, for that matter, throughout the whole book of Amos), we are repeatedly presented with statements such as, "hear the word of the LORD" (v. 16); "this is what the LORD says" (v. 17); or "For the LORD God Almighty declares" (6:14). Amos's message was from God! He had no doubt about it.

> The lion has roared —
> who will not fear?
> The Sovereign LORD has spoken —
> who can but prophesy?
>
> (Amos 3:8)

Whether Amaziah or any other priest, prophet, or king threatened his life, it mattered little to Amos. He was going to be faithful to the task committed to him — to proclaim God's word!

At the heart of Amos's message is the call to live in justice. Amos had a passion for justice. He was a prophet par excellence of justice. Let me now make a brief excursus and say some words about the concept of justice per se.

The Concept of Justice

Justice is a complex concept that is easier to sense than to define. It has multiple definitions according to the many existing schools of thought. Justice, as Karen Lebacqz reminds us, is "a bit like the proverbial elephant examined by blindfolded explorers. Each feels a different part — the foot, the ears, the tusks — and consequently each describes the beast differently — gnarled and tough, thin and supple, smooth and hard. The elephant itself [in this case justice] is not encompassed by any of the individual descriptions."[6]

According to my "touch of the elephant," beyond Aristotle's definition of justice as the virtue of giving and receiving what one is due or what one has a right to — and beyond the valuable contributions of John Rawls or Robert Nozick, among others[7] — there stands the richness of the biblical concept of justice. The Scriptures use various words to speak of justice, but mainly the words *tsedek* and *mishpat* in Hebrew and *dikaiosyne* in Greek. We can translate these words as "righteousness," "judgment," or "justice." Justice as *tsedek*

6. Karen Lebacqz, *Six Theories of Justice: Perspectives from Philosophical and Theological Ethics* (Minneapolis: Augsburg, 1986), p. 9.

7. John Rawls, *A Theory of Justice* (Cambridge, MA: Harvard University Press, 1971); Robert Nozick, *Anarchy, State, and Utopia* (New York: Basic Books, 1974).

speaks about a general living in right relationship with someone, while justice as *mishpat* is somewhat more particular. We can speak of *mishpat* as deciding what is "just" when two people differ or disagree or when one has injured the other.[8] *Dikaiosyne* can have both of these meanings as well.

Furthermore, Scripture teaches that justice is a standard, a plumb line to which all humans must conform in their relationships. Listen to the words of Isaiah 28:17: "I will make justice the measuring line and righteousness the plumb line." Scripture presents us a rich and nuanced understanding of justice. At heart it speaks to us of a concept of justice that I want to underline — that is, justice as "fidelity to the demands of a relationship."[9]

The picture that Scripture paints is that of the human person created *in* and *for* communion — created to live in community. In the Old Testament, above all, one sees the importance of living in relationship with God and with each other. Individuals were in relationship with God through the covenant that existed between God and his people. "As a member of this covenant community, each person was in relationship with every other person, including the poor and needy, one's family, and even with strangers and aliens. Out of these relationships arose responsibilities and de-

8. Lois Barrett, *Doing What Is Right: What the Bible Says about Covenant and Justice* (Scottdale, PA: Herald Press, 1989), p. 21; see also Bruce C. Birch, *Let Justice Roll Down: The Old Testament, Ethics, and Christian Life* (Louisville: Westminster/John Knox Press, 1991), pp. 153-56.

9. John R. Donahue, S.J., "Biblical Perspective on Justice," in *The Faith That Does Justice,* ed. John Haughey (New York: Paulist Press, 1977), p. 68.

mands. The *just* person was faithful to these responsibilities and demands."[10] As Gerhard Von Rad wrote, "There is absolutely no concept in the Old Testament with so central a significance for all relationships of human life as that of *tsedek* [justice]."[11]

Scripture presents justice ultimately as rooted in the righteousness of God. It is grounded in God's holiness and moral character — in God's very being. Our God is just and righteous in God's self and therefore faithful to God's self (as a triune God) and faithful to the demands of God's relationship with all creation. As the psalmist reminds us, "Righteousness and justice are the foundation of your throne" (Ps. 89:14), and "For the LORD is righteous, he loves justice" (Ps. 11:7). Our God is a just God, a faithful God who keeps God's promises. Our God is a God who loves justice — a God who demands justice of all!

Justice in the Book of Amos

The message of the book of Amos can be presented under three basic themes or theological motifs defined by justice, namely: (1) justice among the nations; (2) justice in the nation; and (3) justice and piety of a nation. We will look at each in turn.

10. Bread for the World Educational Fund, "Biblical Basics on Justice," pamphlet (New York: Bread for the World, n.d.), p. 2.

11. Gerhard Von Rad, *Old Testament Theology* (New York: Harper and Bros., 1962), Part I, p. 370, quoted by Donahue, "Biblical Perspective on Justice," p. 68.

1. Justice among the Nations The first two chapters of the book of Amos can be seen as a fascinating presentation of homiletical strategy at its best. It is a psychological-tactical approach that renders the Israelites who are listening to Amos in the marketplace defenseless. Amos begins indicting various nations for their wickedness and injustice, beginning with the nation to the north of Israel (Syria), then moving on to the nations to the west (Philistia and Phoenicia), the south (Edom and Ammon), and the east (Moab), and finally indicting the sister nations, Judah and Israel.

I am sure that one could hear the shouts of "Amen!" as Amos proclaimed, "This is what the LORD says: For three sins of Damascus, even for four, I will not turn back my wrath" (Amos 1:3); "This is what the LORD says: For three sins of Moab, even for four, I will not turn back my wrath" (2:4). But the circle of indictments kept getting closer and closer until the listeners in Israel had no choice but to hear God's clear denunciation of their own sins.

The depth of these indictments, however, is not exhausted by this list of nations, circling ever closer to Amos's listeners. For in these early chapters and throughout the book of Amos we are confronted by the fact that God calls *all* people, *all* nations to account for their behavior. God's standards of justice are universal, for they are rooted in God's righteousness, God's holiness, yes, God's character.

God calls all nations to execute justice. All nations have to give an account of their conduct with other nations. Walter C. Kaiser Jr. puts it this way: "There was no monopoly held by any people, race, or religion on righteousness; justice, goodness, and truth were the standards for all mortals on planet earth or they would have to explain any deviations to Yahweh himself!"[12] Our Lord is a sovereign God over history (Amos 9:7), over creation (5:8), and over the nations (1:3–2:6) — and God demands justice among the nations!

It is important to note that the injustices committed by these nations are similar to the injustices that we tragically see today among the nations. Let me underline a few:

- Damascus (Syria) is accused of cruelty, violence, and atrocities — because she has "threshed Gilead with threshing sledges of iron" (1:3, NRSV).
- Gaza (Philistia) is accused of slave trading — "because she took captive whole communities and sold them" (1:6).
- Tyre (Phoenicia) is accused of breaking a covenant or treaty — "because she . . . disregarded a treaty of brotherhood" (1:9).
- Ammon is accused of imperialism and atrocities — "because he ripped open the pregnant women of Gilead in order to extend his borders" (1:13).

Lamentably, each one of these injustices can be seen in our day and contributes to the reason why we live in times of global crisis:

---

12. Walter C. Kaiser Jr., *Toward Old Testament Ethics* (Grand Rapids: Zondervan, 1983), pp. 12-13.

- Cruelty and violence among nations have been institutionalized and commercialized by the modern "threshing sledges of iron" that represent the lucrative market of weapons or armaments of war, developed by the United States and several nations in Europe and Russia, among others.
- The slave trade is the cruel experience of the Sudan in Africa, where entire ethnic groups are sold in the market. In other cases, just as cruel, young girls and boys are sold into slavery and prostitution by the Asiatic market, among others.
- The breaking of treaties is seen clearly in many nations whose loyalty is dictated, not by covenant or treaty among sovereigns, but by the sovereign and universal globalization of the market. Modern treaties are not worth the paper on which they are written if the "god" Mammon reigns!
- Sad to say, but the (modern) imperialism of the United States, the only existing "super-power" today, has resulted in an increasing unbalance of international power, which, for valid reasons or not, has fomented a more dangerous world — one given to disorder and anarchy.

The people of Israel presumed they were free of the judgment of God because of their privilege as a chosen nation. Nevertheless, Amos reminds them of two vital points. First, he tells them:

Are you not like the Ethiopians [or Nubians] to me,
  O people of Israel? says the LORD.
Did I not bring Israel up from the land of Egypt,
  and the Philistines from Caphtor and the Arameans
    from Kir?

(9:7, NRSV)

The Lord is sovereign in history. Israel, the people of God, has not been the only nation that has experienced liberation. Other nations have experienced their "exodus" by the mighty hand of God.

Second, Amos tells them in the next verse:

Surely the eyes of the Sovereign LORD
  are on the sinful kingdom.
I will destroy it
  from the face of the earth.

(9:8)

The judgment of God is sure. Sooner or later, what the nations sow, that they shall reap. The United States and other nations are not exempt from the consequences of their conduct. God is still sovereign — over creation, over the nations, over history. All must give account for their conduct. God demands justice among the nations. God demands that we live in justice.

2. Justice in the Nation As often happens in the history of nations, political stability and economic prosperity brought about self-sufficiency and indifference among the Israelites. But God placed a "plumb line" in Israel, with equal implications for Judah and for the nations. The "plumb line" revealed a society inclined toward idolatry, oppression, exploitation, and violence — indeed, to injustice. Judgment would come on Israel, for

> They sell the righteous for silver,
>   and the needy for a pair of sandals.
> They trample on the heads of the poor
>   as upon the dust of the ground
>   and deny justice to the oppressed.
>
> (Amos 2:6-7)

It seems that the rich got richer and the poor got poorer. So what's new!

> Hear this word, you cows of Bashan on
>   Mount Samaria,
>   you women who oppress the poor and crush
>   the needy
>   and say to your husbands, "Bring us some drinks!"
>
> (4:1)

Or listen to Amos 5:11:

> You trample on the poor
>   and force him to give you grain.
> Therefore, though you have built stone mansions,

you will not live in them;
though you have planted lush vineyards,
you will not drink their wine.

Injustice was indeed rampant in Israel!

It is critically important for us today to understand that the standard of justice placed before the king and the dominant class (the governor, landowners, business people, judges, and military) is that of *justice toward the poor.* The overwhelming witness of Scripture on the standards and principles (we would say now, "core values") that should guide the rulers of a nation are not issues, for example, that focus on the family per se, or on questionable sexual lifestyles (as important as these are for the health of a nation), but on justice toward the poor and oppressed (see especially Psalm 72). Rulers, and by extension nations, will be judged by how they treat their weakest members — this is the heart of Amos's message. Why is this so? I believe that the teaching of Scripture is clear (in Amos as in the other prophets) that beyond God's intrinsic love and championing for the stranger, widow, poor, and needy lies also the reality of idolatry. As the commandments teach us: "I am the LORD your God. . . . You shall have no other gods before me . . . for I, the LORD your God, am a jealous God" (Exod. 20:1-5).

While many of the Israelites may not have worshiped idols of wood or rock (as many may not today), yet they rendered "worship" to the god of wealth *(Mammon).* The desire and anxiety for riches, an obsessive note in the lives of the dominant class, led to their oppression of the poor and needy and the corruption of the courts, the market, the religious system, and the society at large. Washington Padilla reminds us that a central note of Amos was of "social injustice as the specific form that the sin of idolatry assumes in society."[13] The lesson is clear: idolatry is at the heart of social injustice and the eventual downfall of a nation. Social injustice, not sexual immorality per se, is the central criterion by which to judge a ruler or nation (see Ezek. 16:49-50).

Our nation is at a critical juncture in history. In his book *The Twilight of American Culture*, Morris Berman underlines, among other things, that one of the factors accompanying the decline of American civilization is accelerating social and economic inequality. He states that, "in terms of wealth disparity, the United States leads all other major industrial nations."[14] Furthermore, quoting David Rieff of the World Policy Institute, he declares, "America, with its widening income gap, its vast, deepening divergences in everything from education to life expectancy between rich and poor, is less democratic today . . . than it was in 1950."[15] The call of the prophet Amos, then as now, is the same:

13. Padilla, *Amós-Abdías*, p. 14.

14. Morris Berman, *The Twilight of American Culture* (New York: W. W. Norton, 2000), p. 21.

15. Berman, *The Twilight of American Culture*, p. 23. See also Genaro C. Armas, "Wealth Gap Broadened, Study Says," *The Boston Globe*, October 18, 2004, p. A-2. Eileen McNamara asks the question: "Why no outrage about the fact that the top 1 percent earns more than the bottom 40 percent in the United States, the widest income gap since 1929?" in "Inoffensive, Ineffective," *The Boston Globe*, November 7, 2004, p. B-1.

But let justice roll on like a river,
righteousness like a never-failing stream!

(Amos 5:24)

If our nation — for that matter, our world — is to hear the whole Word of God, we must do away with those false dichotomies that would limit the Word of God and define the gospel as *either* evangelism *or* social justice. We have come a long way in this area, but much more needs to be done. We must completely reverse the reversal of the early twentieth-century American church, which divided the church into two camps. A few years ago this was described well by Paul S. Rees in an article entitled "Freeing up":

> By and large, the evangelicals abdicated. They left it to the naughty "liberals" to get involved with the issues of poverty and hunger, racial discrimination and the subversion of civil rights, the exploitation of children and women, war and peace. It was a distressful situation. On one hand were masses of Christians who scorned the "personal gospel" to exalt the "social." On the other hand were masses of Christians who spurned the "social" to exalt the "personal." And all the while there has been in fact *only one gospel*. The good news of salvation in Christ must be verified personally and it must be validated socially.[16]

16. Paul S. Rees, "Freeing Up," *World Vision*, April 1982 (my emphasis).

God is concerned for the whole person. Ours is a holistic gospel, responding to the whole needs of the person. A central concern in the book of Amos, and in all the biblical teaching about society, is that God has a passionate concern for justice for all — especially the poor, the weak, and the oppressed members of society. God demands justice in the nation!

3. Justice and Piety of a Nation The Israelites had forsaken the needy and oppressed. They pretended to worship the true God by the multitude of their offerings and gifts. They even excelled in the composing of music for temple worship. There was a form of revival — yes, the temples were crowded ("a true mega-church") — yet it was an abomination to God. Theirs was a formalism that stunk! Listen to God's words:

> I hate, I despise your religious feasts;
>   I cannot stand your assemblies.
> Even though you bring me burnt offerings and
>   grain offerings,
>   I will not accept them.
> Though you bring choice fellowship offerings,
>   I will have no regard for them.
> Away with the noise of your songs!
>   I will not listen to the music of your harps.
> But let justice roll on like a river
>   righteousness like a never-failing stream!
>
> (Amos 5:21-24)

Throughout Scripture we can find important truths about worship that relate authentic worship to our behavior toward the poor and oppressed. The words of Amos are "echoed" by the prophet Isaiah when he says:

> Is such the fast that I choose,
>   a day to humble oneself?
> Is it to bow down the head like a bulrush,
>   and to lie in sackcloth and ashes?
> Will you call this a fast,
>   a day acceptable to the LORD?
> Is not this the fast I choose:
>   to loose the bonds of injustice . . .
> to let the oppressed go free . . . ?
> Is it not to share your bread with the hungry,
>   and bring the homeless poor into your house;
> when you see the naked, to cover them,
>   and not to hide yourself from your own kin?
>
> (Isa. 58:5-7; NRSV)

The "fast" of the people of God here represents that form of spirituality or worship that believes God is impressed by the ritual sacrifice of our religiosity (in itself a formalism), without the presence of justice toward the poor! The fasting or worship that pleases our God is accompanied by acts of mercy and justice toward the poor, the broken, and the oppressed. Furthermore, such true worship has the great promises of God's blessings.

The prophet Isaiah continues:

Then your light shall break forth like the dawn,
   and your healing shall spring up quickly;
your vindicator shall go before you,
   the glory of the LORD shall be your rearguard.
Then you shall call, and the LORD will answer. . . .
The LORD will guide you continually,
   and satisfy your needs in parched places,
   and make your bones strong;
and you shall be like a watered garden,
   like a spring of water,
   whose waters never fail.

(Isa. 58:8-9, 11; NRSV)

In God's economy, worship with justice or justice with worship *equals* God's blessing!

There is a seamless relationship between ethical behavior and true worship, between justice and piety. Who we are and how we behave are intimately related in our giving *worth* to our God. For true worship, whether expressed in our daily walk or in a building called a temple or church, must be "in spirit and truth" (John 4:23). In the New Testament, for example, we find these profound and disturbing words in Matthew 25:42-45:

"For I was hungry and you gave me nothing to eat, I was thirsty and you gave me nothing to drink, I was a stranger and you did not invite me in, I needed clothes and you did not clothe me, I was sick and in prison and you did not look after me." They also will answer, "Lord, when did we see you hungry or thirsty or a stranger or needing clothes or sick or in prison, and did not help you?" He will reply, "I tell you the truth, whatever you did not do for one of the least of these, you did not do for me."

There is a great mystery here, for as we give and serve with justice the poor and needy in our midst, we are in a deep yet spiritually profound sense doing it to the Lord — we are ascribing *worth* to our Lord, we are worshiping him. May our worship be in spirit and in truth. May we in our worship live in justice. Amos was a leader with a sure word from God. May we be sure of faithfully proclaiming the whole Word of God!

Singular Courage from God

Let me conclude with some brief remarks on the third indispensable quality of a minister of the Word of God. It docsn't take much to see from our autobiographical passage that Amos was a man of great courage. Not only was he a man from Judah preaching in Israel, but he was preaching in "the king's sanctuary and the temple of the kingdom" (Amos 7:13). He was a threat to the political establishment as well as to the religious establishment represented by Amaziah. Yet Amos would not be intimidated or bribed. He had a message from God, and he had to proclaim it! Amos's words were tough, though I'm sure they were spoken from a broken heart. He focused on God's justice.

Whether the messenger is Martin Luther or Martin Luther King Jr., God's message of justice will always demand courage of its messengers. But we can, nay, we must do no less than courageously challenge *all* to live in justice. While it is important to look closely at the reason why God judges the nations and Israel — especially since our world is in many ways so similar to the one Amos observed — it is also important to remember the positive side of that judgment: "Those whom I [the Lord] love I rebuke and discipline" (Rev. 3:19). God's severity was a proof of God's desire to discipline and purify God's people, whom God loved. "For the LORD is righteous, he loves justice" (Ps. 11:7).

Amos responded to the call of God in his life. I believe that as he stepped out in faith in the word of God, and as he uncompromisingly proclaimed its message, that word provided the strength and courage to carry on. In those dark days and moments when doubt, intimidation, and fear would overtake Amos — and they do come to all who would faithfully serve the word of God — Amos, I am sure, cried out, like Jeremiah:

> But if I say, "I will not mention him
>   or speak any more in his name,"
> his word is in my heart like a burning fire,
>   shut up in my bones.
> I am weary of holding it in;
>   indeed, I cannot.
>
> (Jer. 20:9)

We live in times that demand intrepid ministers of the Word of God. Amos was such a man. May we have a strong sense of God's calling; may we have a sure word from God; may we proclaim that word and live in justice; and may we have singular courage to carry on until he comes. "Even so, come, Lord Jesus."

Let me conclude with a "Franciscan Benediction":

May God bless you with *discomfort* at easy answers, half-truths, and superficial relationships, so that you may live deep within your heart.

May God bless you with *anger* at injustice, oppression, and exploitation of people, so that you may work for justice, freedom, and peace.

May God bless you with *tears* to shed for those who suffer from pain, rejection, starvation, and war, so that you may reach out your hand to comfort them and to turn their pain into joy.

And may God bless you with enough *foolishness* to believe that you can make a difference in this world, so that you can do what others claim cannot be done.

A RESPONSE TO

"Amos, Intrepid Leader for Justice"

Veli-Mattí Kärkkäinen

It is an extraordinary honor and joy to offer some theological reflections on this excellent and challenging presentation by Dr. Eldin Villafañe. The same quality of biblical, theological, ethical, and sociocultural expertise was evident in this lecture as is evident in everything this leading evangelical ethicist and urban ministry specialist does. Many of us are familiar with several of his seminal publications. My own introduction to Dr. Villafañe's work came through reading with enthusiasm his book titled *The Liberating Spirit*.[1]

My task as respondent is both rewarding and humbling. It is rewarding in that a passionate presentation such as the one under discussion inspires theological and missiological reflections in so many directions. The task is humbling in

---

1. Eldin Villafañe, *The Liberating Spirit: Toward an Hispanic American Pentecostal Social Ethic* (Grand Rapids: Eerdmans, 1993).

that there is so little — if anything — to critique. Often respondents glory in being able to show the fallacy of the presentation, or at least point to several key ideas where the author was less than convincing. In this case, there are none. My overall response to the presentation is short and powerful: "Amen." There is nothing I need to disagree with and very little I could possibly add to it.

Yet, as mentioned, a challenging presentation such as this also gives an opportunity to continue reflections and perhaps highlight perspectives that the presenter could not touch in the confines of one paper. So take my comments here as extended footnotes or, as was usual in medieval theology, as comments in the margin of the text. As such they invite both the presenter and the audience to continue thinking about the theology of justice from the perspective Dr. Villafañe has opened for us.

I find it quite interesting and exciting that out of all prophetic figures available in the Old Testament — all of whom were spokespersons for Yahweh and Yahweh's justice in their own way — Dr. Villafañe chose Amos, the first writing prophet. This was an intelligent and thoughtful choice. Commonalities between the time of Amos and our own time — as the presentation hints — are not to be easily dismissed. Just think of the many similarities between Israel, the then northern state to which Amos traveled from his home in Judah, and the affluent West in which we find ourselves in the beginning of a new millennium. By the mid-eighth century B.C., Jeroboam II, Israel's king, had been able to bring about unprecedented prosperity. Israelite agriculture flourished, as the fourth chapter of Amos indicates (4:6-9), and the stock market was on the rise. While not devoid of potential conflicts, the international scene was peaceful. Yes, there were threats — just read the masterful speeches of judgment in the first two chapters of the book of Amos and you will find the surrounding nations — but there was a feeling of security, if not complacency. Israel took comfort in its military power, as 6:13, for example, illustrates. There was also a trend of urbanization, not unlike in the City of Angels or any other major city on the globe today.

Not only that, but religion was on the rise — as Dr. Villafañe's paper notes. Religion sold (Amos 2:8), and temples were filled with enthusiastic worshipers (5:21-24). Yet at the same time there was exploitation of the needy and lack of concern for the poor and underprivileged.

As an ethicist and urban minister, Dr. Villafañe has masterfully analyzed the contemporary scene at the national and international levels — so woefully similar to the picture Amos paints. To combat the complacency and indifference among Christian churches in general and evangelical churches in particular, Dr. Villafañe has called for a holistic gospel.

This, I believe, is an essential task for all of us. As long as social concern and love for the poor, oppressed, and needy are optional, an appendix to the gospel, nothing much may happen in evangelical churches. While non-evangelical churches don't necessarily have a more glorious track record when it comes to doing justice — and not just speaking about it — at least some of them have grasped the theological significance of justice in the gospel. For example, the Roman Catholic Church in the aftermath of Vatican II has come to speak of justice and social concern as constitutive for the gospel. This means that there is no "full gospel" without attention to the ethical and social aspects so clearly spelled out in the Word of God. The one who wants to preach the full gospel, the unadulterated Word of God, is bound to read Amos, Isaiah, and other spokespersons for justice — as well as the Sermon on the Mount and many other teachings of our Lord and Savior — as the true Word of God. In order for our *devotionals* to become meaningful, we need to *devote* ourselves to the cause of God.

Among the many key insights in Dr. Villafañe's paper, there was one in particular that struck me with its far-reaching theological potential. It had to do with the clarification of the biblical meaning of the concept of justice and especially its connection to the idea of relationality. Justice is related to the faithfulness of Yahweh and his covenant relationship with his people. Could that idea be connected with the contemporary consensus on trinitarian doctrine, which operates so much with the idea of relationality and community? Could new light be shed on the concept of justice and covenant from the perspective of God as communion? God is relational in the inner-trinitarian relationships — eternal, equal, yet interdependent — and is likewise relational in God's relation to creation and to God's people, as Dr. Villafañe so helpfully explained.

This is, of course, not a novel idea. Some liberation theologians have made use of it, especially in the Latin

American context, including Leonardo Boff. In his *Trinity and Society* he argues that the relationality and communion in the godhead should be our "social program."[2] I would be excited to hear more from Dr. Villafañe along these lines.

Another subject that I would like to hear more on has to do with identification with the poor. Dr. Villafañe argues that Amos — himself coming from poverty as a rural worker who had to take on an extra job to support himself — was able to identify with the poor. So far so good. However, the picture changes if, with many Old Testament scholars, we happen to take another stance in this much disputed question concerning Amos's occupation — or the nature of his occupation, to be more precise. What if the preacher of justice did not come from underprivileged conditions, but rather was a quite well-to-do agricultural professional, maybe even a kind of "consultant" who had a chance to travel, a privilege rare at that time? Since I am not a biblical scholar (nor is Old Testament criticism Dr. Villafañe's main area), I am less interested in this question for the sake of historical accuracy and more for the sake of understanding how one's social location may influence one's theology of social concern. It is a question that evangelicalism should address.

Another constellation of questions in my mind about which I would love to hear more from Dr. Villafañe has to do with his spiritual background, namely Pentecostalism, a

2. Leonardo Boff, *Trinity and Society* (Maryknoll, NY: Orbis Books, 1988).

Christian family that has also nurtured, and continues to nurture, my own life. Let us suppose this paper had been presented to a primarily Pentecostal audience; would it have to be different or not? We could also ask, what, if any, are the resources and the challenges that come from that particular Christian tradition? In *The Liberating Spirit,* Dr. Villafañe's Pentecostal location is more evident, and there is a lot in this discussion that is highly interesting to all of us, especially in a community such as Fuller, which embraces students and faculty from all Christian churches.

As an aside, let me remark that there are striking parallels between Amos, the intrepid leader for justice, and the typical Pentecostal preacher. Both claim to be non-professionals (however one solves the difficult translation problem of 7:14, it seems clear enough that Amos did not come from a prophet school or identify himself with official prophetic status). Like Amos, who echoed the unexpected call of King David of old, who was "taken away from the flock," the Pentecostal preacher attributes his or her spiritual authority not to divinity school or books but to divine appointment. Both Amos and the Pentecostal preacher have a strong sense of calling, and they often — especially in the contexts outside of the affluent West — find themselves in the margins and over against the power structures.

When reflecting on the Pentecostal implications of Dr. Villafañe's call for social justice, I noticed that, while he uses the short book of Amos quite widely, there is one section totally untouched, and that is the ending of the book, the latter part of chapter 9. Here is the famous eschatological promise of the reversal of roles, clothed in typical Old Testament imagery of a transformational renewal of creation:

"The days are coming," declares the LORD,
"when the reaper will be overtaken by the plowman
and the planter by the one treading grapes.
New wine will drip from the mountains
and flow from all the hills."

(Amos 9:13)

While these verses probably come from a later hand, as most scholars agree, the role of this eschatological promise is significant and instructive. Unlike for many evangelicals and Pentecostals, for Amos the radical eschatological hope did not make efforts to improve social conditions any less important. In fact, perhaps the opposite was the case: knowing that Yahweh will bring about the kingdom of *shalom,* there was confidence in the "social program." Yahweh invites the people to participate in the coming of the time of peace and justice, even though that entails radical divine intervention. How would the theme of eschatology and social justice inform an intrepid leader who yearns to preach the full gospel?

Here at Fuller there has been a lot of talk about the meaning of the gospel. It all started a few years ago when we started wondering if our teaching at Fuller and our chapel services really reflect the holistic gospel of the Word of God, or if they are rather an expression of our own evangelical wishful religious thinking. We do not yet know much more about the meaning of the gospel, but extended discussions among the faculty at various levels and a series of sermons in chapel services have at least woken us up. We are not satisfied with the individualistic, "spiritualist," "feel good," often escapist Western/evangelical notion of the gospel. We want to go back to our "sources" and claim the full gospel. No doubt Dr. Villafañe has come to speak to us at an opportune time; his messages have reminded us of the importance of not only hearing but also doing the gospel, the Word of God.

Bibliography

Abraham, William J. *The Logic of Renewal*. Grand Rapids: Eerdmans, 2003.

Agosto, Efraín. "Paul vs. Empire: A Postcolonial and Latino Reading of Philippians." *PERSPECTIVAS*, Occasional Papers, Fall 2002.

Anderson, Walter. *Reality Isn't What It Used to Be*. San Francisco: Harper and Row, 1990.

Bainton, Roland H. *Here I Stand: A Life of Martin Luther*. New York: Abingdon Press, 1950.

Banks, Robert. *Reenvisioning Theological Education: Exploring a Missional Alternative to Current Models*. Grand Rapids: Eerdmans, 1999.

Barrett, Lois. *Doing What Is Right: What the Bible Says about Covenant and Justice*. Scottdale, PA: Herald Press, 1989.

Barth, Karl. *The Call to Discipleship*. Minneapolis: Fortress Press, 2003.

————. "The Christian Community and the Civil Community." In *Against the Stream*. London: SCM Press, 1934.

————. *Church Dogmatics*. Edited by T. F. Torrance and Geoffrey W. Bromiley. Edinburgh: T. & T. Clark, 1956-1975.

————. *The Epistle to the Philippians*. Atlanta: John Knox Press, 1962.

————. *The Humanity of God*. Atlanta: John Knox Press, 1976.

Bauckham, Richard. *Bible and Mission: Christian Witness in a Postmodern World*. Grand Rapids: Baker Academic, 2003.

Bauman, Zygmunt. *Life in Fragments: Essays in Postmodern Morality*. Oxford: Blackwell, 1995.

————. *Postmodern Ethics*. Oxford: Blackwell, 1993.

Beaudoin, Tom. *Virtual Faith: The Irreverent Spiritual Quest of Generation X*. San Francisco: Jossey-Bass, 1998.

Berman, Morris. *The Twilight of American Culture*. New York: W. W. Norton, 2000.

Berquist, Jon L. *Incarnation*. St. Louis: Chalice Press, 1999.

Birch, Bruce C. *Let Justice Roll Down: The Old Testament, Ethics, and Christian Life*. Louisville: Westminster/John Knox Press, 1991.

Boff, Leonardo. *Trinity and Society*. Maryknoll, NY: Orbis Books, 1988.

Bonhoeffer, Dietrich. *The Cost of Discipleship*. New York: Touchstone, 1995.

Borgmann, Albert. *Crossing the Postmodern Divide*. Chicago: University of Chicago Press, 1992.

Bread for the World Educational Fund. "Biblical Basics on Justice." Pamphlet. New York: Bread for the World, n.d.

Carroll R., Mark Daniel. *Contexts for Amos: Prophetic Poetics in Latin American Perspective*. Sheffield: Sheffield Academic Press, 1992.

Donahue, John R., S.J. "Biblical Perspective on Justice." In *The*

Faith That Does Justice, ed. John Haughey. New York: Paulist Press, 1977.

Engel, James F., and William A. Dyrness. *Changing the Mind of Missions: Where Have We Gone Wrong?* Downers Grove, IL: InterVarsity Press, 2000.

Erickson, Millard J. *Christian Theology.* 2nd edition. Grand Rapids: Baker Books, 1999.

Fackre, Gabriel. *The Christian Story: A Narrative Interpretation of Basic Christian Doctrine.* Grand Rapids: Eerdmans, 1984.

Farley, Edward. *Theologia: The Fragmentation and Unity of Theological Education.* Philadelphia: Fortress, 1983.

Fee, Gordon. *Paul's Letter to the Philippians.* New International Commentary on the New Testament. Grand Rapids: Eerdmans, 1991.

————. "Philippians 2:5-11: Hymn or Exalted Pauline Prose?" *Bulletin for Biblical Research* 2 (1992).

Feinberg, Paul D. "The *Kenosis* and Christology: An Exegetical-Theological Analysis of Phil. 2:6-11." *Trinity Journal* 1 (1980).

Gallup, George, Jr., and Timothy Jones. *The Next American Spirituality: Finding God in the Twenty-First Century.* Colorado Springs, CO: Chariot Victor Publishing, 2000.

González, Justo L. "Metamodern Aliens in Postmodern Jerusalem." In *Hispanic/Latino Theology: Challenge and Promise,* ed. Ada María Isasi-Díaz and Fernando F. Segovia. Minneapolis: Fortress Press, 1996.

————. "Encarnación e Historia." In *Fe Cristiana y Latinoamérica Hoy,* ed. C. René Padilla. Buenos Aires: Ediciones Certeza, 1974.

————. "And the Word Was Made Flesh." In *Mañana: Chris-*

tian Theology from a Hispanic Perspective. Nashville: Abingdon Press, 1990.

————. "The Christological Debates to the Council of Chalcedon." In *The Story of Christianity: The Early Church to the Dawn of the Reformation*. Volume 1. New York: Harper & Row, 1984.

————. *A History of Christian Thought: From the Beginnings to the Council of Chalcedon*. Volume 1. Revised edition. Nashville: Abingdon Press, 1987.

Gorman, Michael J. *Cruciformity: Paul's Narrative Spirituality of the Cross*. Grand Rapids: Eerdmans, 2001.

Grenz, Stanley J. *A Primer on Postmodernism*. Grand Rapids: Eerdmans, 1996.

Guder, Darrell L. *The Incarnation and the Church's Witness*. Harrisburg, PA: Trinity Press International, 1999.

Kaiser, Walter C., Jr. *Toward Old Testament Ethics*. Grand Rapids: Zondervan, 1983.

Kelsey, David. *Between Athens and Berlin: The Theological Education Debate*. Philadelphia: Fortress, 1983.

Lebacqz, Karen. *Six Theories of Justice: Perspectives from Philosophical and Theological Ethics*. Minneapolis: Augsburg, 1986.

Lehmann, Paul. *Ethics in a Christian Context*. New York: Harper & Row, 1963.

Lyotard, Jean-François. *The Postmodern Condition: A Report on Knowledge*. Minneapolis: University of Minnesota Press, 1984.

Mays, James L. *Amos: A Commentary*. Philadelphia: Westminster, 1969.

Meeks, Wayne A. "The Man from Heaven in Paul's Letter to the Philippians." In *The Future of Early Christianity: Essays in Honor of Helmut Koester,* ed. Birger Pearson. Minneapolis: Fortress Press, 1991.

Messer, Donald E. *Calling Church and Seminary into the Twenty-First Century.* Nashville: Abingdon Press, 1995.

Nozick, Robert. *Anarchy, State, and Utopia.* New York: Basic Books, 1974.

O'Brien, Peter. *Commentary on Philippians.* New International Greek Testament Commentary. Grand Rapids: Eerdmans, 1991.

Padilla, Washington. *Amós-Abdías.* Comentario Biblico Hispanoamericano. Miami: Editorial Caribe, 1989.

Pagán, Samuel. "Entonces vi . . . una tierra nueva: De la modernidad a la postmodernidad en la iglesia hispana." *APUNTES* 20, no. 4 (2000).

Pagitt, Doug. *Reimagining Spiritual Formation: A Week in the Life of an Experimental Church.* Grand Rapids: Zondervan, 2004.

Pazmiño, Roberto. *Foundational Issues in Christian Education: An Introduction in Evangelical Perspective.* Grand Rapids: Baker Book House, 1988.

Peace, Richard V. *Conversion in the New Testament: Paul and the Twelve.* Grand Rapids: Eerdmans, 1999.

Pedraja, Luis. *Jesus Is My Uncle: Christology from a Hispanic Perspective.* Nashville: Abingdon Press, 1999.

Poe, Harry Lee. *Christian Witness in a Postmodern World.* Nashville: Abingdon Press, 2001.

Rawls, John. *A Theory of Justice.* Cambridge, MA: Harvard University Press, 1971.

Rees, Paul S. "Freeing Up." *World Vision,* April 1982.

Sanders, Jack T. *The New Testament Christological Hymns.* Cambridge: Cambridge University Press, 1971.

Silva, Moisés. *Philippians*. Baker Exegetical Commentary on the New Testament. Grand Rapids: Baker Book House, 1992.

Sobrino, Jon. "La Cristología Conciliar." In *La Fe en Jesucristo: Ensayo desde las víctimas*. Madrid: Editorial Trotta, 1999.

Solzhenitsyn, Aleksandr I. *The Gulag Archipelago 1918-1956*. New York: Harper Collins, 1985.

St. Athanasius. *On the Incarnation: The Treatise De Incarnatione Verbi Dei*. Crestwood, NY: St. Vladimir's Seminary Press, 2000.

Stuart, Douglas. *Hosea-Jonah*. Word Biblical Commentary 31. Waco, TX: Word, 1987.

Tracy, David. "A Social Portrait of the Theologian — The Three Publics of Theology: Society, Academy and Church." In *The Analogical Imagination: Christian Thought and the Culture of Pluralism*. New York: Crossroad, 1981.

Unamuno, Miguel De. *El Cristo de Velázquez* (Poema). Madrid: Esposa-Calpe, 1967.

Villafañe, Eldin. "A Prayer for the City: Paul's Benediction and a Vision for Urban Theological Education." In *A Prayer for the City: Further Reflections on Urban Ministry*. Austin, TX: AETH, 2001.

———. *The Liberating Spirit: Toward an Hispanic American Pentecostal Social Ethic*. Grand Rapids: Eerdmans, 1993.

Villafañe, Eldin, Bruce W. Jackson, Robert A. Evans, and Alice Frazer Evans. *Transforming the City: Reframing Education for Urban Ministry*. Grand Rapids: Eerdmans, 2002.

Von Rad, Gerhard. *Old Testament Theology*. New York: Harper and Bros., 1962.

Wolff, Hans W. *Joel and Amos*. Hermeneia. Philadelphia: Fortress, 1977.

Contributors

VELI-MATTÍ KÄRKKÄINEN (Dr. Theol., University of Helsinki; Dr. Theol., Habil., University of Helsinki) is professor of systematic theology at Fuller Theological Seminary. He served as president and professor at IsoKirja College in Keuruu, Finland, and docent of ecumenics at the University of Helsinki. His teaching and research experience includes Finland, Thailand, and the United States, as well as Visiting Lectureships in Croatia, Russia, and Egypt. Among his many books are *Pneumatology: The Holy Spirit in Ecumenical, International, and Contextual Perspective* and *An Introduction to the Theology of Religions: Biblical, Historical and Contemporary Perspective*. Dr. Kärkkäinen is a member of three working groups of the World Council of Churches and has participated in numerous international consultations.

HOWARD J. LOEWEN (Ph.D., Fuller Theological Seminary) is dean of the School of Theology and professor of theology and ethics at Fuller Theological Seminary. He has served as provost of Fresno Pacific University and as academic dean and professor of theology at Mennonite Brethren Biblical Seminary. Dr. Loewen has been a visiting scholar at the Graduate Theological Union and the University of Edinburgh. He has held teaching positions at Fuller Theological Seminary, Concord College, Mennonite Brethren Biblical Seminary, and Fresno Pacific University. Among his theological works is *One Lord, One Church, One Hope, and One God: Mennonite Confessions of Faith in North America.* He has also served several congregations in teaching and pastoral roles. Dr. Loewen has been involved extensively in ecumenical dialogues and in international educational ministries.

JUAN FRANCISCO MARTINEZ (Ph.D., Fuller Theological Seminary) is director of the Hispanic church studies department and assistant professor of Hispanic studies and pastoral leadership at Fuller Theological Seminary. He formerly served as the rector of the Latin American Anabaptist Seminary in Guatemala City, Guatemala. A Mennonite pastor, Dr. Martinez also has experience in church planting and teaching in both religious and secular venues. He served as director of Hispanic ministries for the Pacific District Conference of the Mennonite Brethren Church. Dr. Martinez has published articles in several journals in both English and Spanish and is coeditor with Luis Scott of *Iglesias peregrinas en busca de identidad: Cuadros del protestantismo Latino en los Estados Unidos.*

RICHARD PEACE (Ph.D., University of Natal) is the Robert Boyd Munger Professor of Evangelism and Spiritual Formation at Fuller Theological Seminary. An ordained minister in the United Church of Christ, Dr. Peace is a consultant in church growth and small-group training. As a former freelance documentary filmmaker, he serves as a consultant in media productions and educational design for groups ranging from the Navigators in Colorado Springs to the Centers for Disease Control in Atlanta. He is also the author of numerous publications, including *Small Group Evangelism* and the *Learning to Love* and *Spiritual Disciplines* series. Dr. Peace's most recent book is *Conversion in the New Testament: Paul and the Twelve.*